Kevin Lane Dunn

£PBC
$3
9-21

# PRIVATE THEATRICALS

# · PRIVATE ·
# THEATRICALS

## The Lives of the Victorians

## NINA AUERBACH

HARVARD UNIVERSITY PRESS

CAMBRIDGE, MASSACHUSETTS

LONDON, ENGLAND

1990

*Library of Congress Cataloging-in-Publication Data*
Auerbach, Nina, 1943–
   Private theatricals : the lives of the Victorians / Nina Auerbach.
      p.   cm.
   Includes bibliographical references.
   ISBN 0–674–70755–9 (alk. paper)
   1. Theater—Great Britain—History—19th century. 2. English
drama—19th century—History and criticism. 3. Illusion in
literature. 4. Role playing in literature. I. Title.
PN2594.A8 1990                                        89–20045
792'.0941'09034—dc20                    ·                    CIP

*For Carl R. Woodring*

# · ACKNOWLEDGMENTS ·

This account of theatricality combines three fields of inquiry that are traditionally segregated from each other: theater history, literary criticism, and the history of culture. Arbitrary academic conventions have isolated the Victorian theater from supposedly nontheatrical literary culture; restoring the theater to its central, pervasive place in the Victorian imagination was a particularly intense and gratifying challenge.

Most of this book was written in Philadelphia, but it began in Princeton and ended in Seattle. Its scenic and inclusive journey gave it helpers and friends from several different fields. *Private Theatricals* first found an audience in October 1986, as a series of three Christian Gauss Seminars at Princeton University. Victor Brombert and Ulrich Knoepflmacher made me feel particularly welcome in Princeton, but I should like to thank all relevant committee members who invited me to present the Christian Gauss Seminars, my companions at the stimulating dinners that preceded my presentations, and especially, the lively, interdisciplinary audience of Princetonians and others whose challenging questions helped transmute my lectures from work-in-progress to finished book. The spectacle of a Princeton autumn was almost as great a stimulus to my ideas about theatricality as were our more formal academic exchanges.

The University of Washington gave my life and work an even more spectacular transformation when I moved to Seattle to become the Solomon Katz Distinguished Visiting Professor in the

## Acknowledgments

Humanities in the spring of 1989. Seattle's incomparable blend of nature and night life provided a perfect setting for the completion of *Private Theatricals*. The enthusiasm of my graduate students at the University of Washington for the theater and theatrical perceptions made finishing this book a joy. The lively, friendly community at the university provided an instant home; I am particularly grateful to Sue-Ellen Case, Richard Dunn, and Kathleen Blake for their many contributions, practical, social, and intangible, to my new life and this book.

David J. DeLaura, Chair of my home department at the University of Pennsylvania, provided the most important help of all: a sabbatical leave allowing time in which to think and write. Colin Blake, Jennifer Brody, Victor Brombert, Carl Dawson, Beth Kalikoff, Ulrich Knoepflmacher, Jacob Korg, Cary M. Mazer, Karen Neff, Judith Pascoe, Phyllis and Donald Rackin, and Carole Silver made wonderfully helpful suggestions and, in some cases, gifts of material that enriched my work immeasurably. Kathleen Blake and Cary M. Mazer read an almost-completed draft and were infallibly shrewd in locating areas of my argument I had smudged or works I had overlooked. Any remaining smudges or omissions are solely my responsibility.

I am particularly grateful to Georgianna Ziegler, Curator of the Furness Library at the University of Pennsylvania, for her uncanny assistance in finding exactly the right illustrations.

Finally, this book is one dramatization of my debt to Carl R. Woodring, to whom it is dedicated. Carl R. Woodring has introduced many of us to the breadth and flexibility of nineteenth-century culture. What may be more important still, his own unobtrusive theatricality has exemplified over the years a lack of submission to fixed ideas, even those ideas we will resolutely to believe in.

N.A.

Seattle, 1989

# · CONTENTS ·

· ix ·

# PRIVATE THEATRICALS

## · INTRODUCTION ·

# *Trees and Transfigurations*

## Natural Lives

This book is about Victorian men and women who had nothing left to believe in but their lives. The loss of faith that sages mourned was in part a loss of humanized time: surveying prehuman history, nineteenth-century geologists posited an infinity so vast that it consumed the human scale. In compensation, Carlyle and his followers exhorted readers to believe that "a whole epitome of the Infinite, with its meanings, lies enfolded in the Life of Every Man."[1] Birth acquired the authority of lost Edenic origins; death gained the conclusiveness attributed to the Last Judgment. Because the shape of lives took on the spiritual authority the universe withheld, Victorians—even many of the women Carlyle's benediction excluded—strained to believe that lives were in truth "epitomes of the Infinite."

Refuting Charles Kingsley's accusation that he was a liar, John Henry Newman responded with his age's truth as well as his own, the story of his life: "I must show what I am, that it may be seen what I am not, and that the phantom may be extinguished which gibbers instead of me. I wish to be known as a living man, and not as a scarecrow which is dressed up in my clothes."[2] The "living man," not his beliefs, is the only weapon powerful enough to prevail against imputed dishonesty. In Newman's spirit of salvation, the ecstatic young David of Robert Browning's *Saul* tries to heal his king with a quintessential Victorian celebration of a "living man" in all his sacramental glory: "How good is man's life, the mere living! how fit to employ / All the heart and the soul and the senses forever in joy!" (*Saul*, 1845–1855, ll. 78–79).

Saul, like many Victorians, remained unconsoled. But if "the mere living" did not fully engage faith "forever in joy," it *was* verifiable; it would not disappear into the void of science.

As sources of truth, though, lives could be dangerously like masks. Living was so significant that sages strained to shelter it from contamination; the theater became the primary source and metaphor for meretricious, life-destroying activity. The *OED* enlists Carlyle's *French Revolution* for its first entry under "theatricality": "By act and word he strives to do it; with sincerity, if possible; failing that, with theatricality." "Theatricality" is such a rich and fearful word in Victorian culture that it is most accurately defined, as Carlyle uses it, in relation to the pure things it is not. Sincerity is sanctified and it is not sincere.

Reverent Victorians shunned theatricality as the ultimate, deceitful mobility. It connotes not only lies, but a fluidity of character that decomposes the uniform integrity of the self. The idea that character might be inherently unstable—that Newman's "phantom . . . which gibbers instead of me" might also be the real man—is so unnerving that Victorian literature conveys a covert fear that any activity is destructive of character because all activity smacks of acting. The fear of performance that pervades nineteenth-century humanism finds its epitome in the immobility of the Victorian Shakespeare. As Carlyle's heroic man of letters, Shakespeare does not have to write plays: he secretes them out of his grandeur.

> Such a man's works, whatsoever he with utmost conscious exertion and forethought shall accomplish, grow up withal *un*consciously, from the unknown deeps in him;—as the oak-tree grows from the Earth's bosom, as the mountains and waters shape themselves; with a symmetry grounded on Nature's own laws, conformable to all Truths whatsoever. How much in Shakespeare lies hid; his sorrows, his silent struggles known to himself; much that was not known at all, not speakable at all; like *roots*, like sap and forces working underground! Speech is great; but Silence is greater.[3]

It makes little immediate sense to praise the most volubly mercurial of playwrights for his silence and to endow him with the immobility of a tree. This Shakespeare belongs to nature, not theater; he is revered for his roots, not his words. He is like a god, not because he speaks divinely but because he is only quasi-articulate. His talents, actions, achievements, fade into his enigmatic presence.

In the same spirit, George Eliot's first hero—the Christ she created as Mary Ann Evans, anonymous translator of David Friedrich Strauss's *Das Leben Jesu*—is shorn of miracles and miraculous spiritual insights. As with Carlyle's silenced Shakespeare, only Christ's dimly discerned life is worthy of remembrance: "Historically, Jesus can have been nothing more than a person, highly distinguished indeed, but subject to the limitations inevitable to all that is mortal: by means of his exalted character, however, he exerted so powerful an influence over the religious sentiment, that it constituted him the ideal of piety; in accordance with the general rule, that an historical fact or person cannot become the basis of a positive religion until it is elevated into the sphere of the ideal."[4]

Like Eliot's novels, the relentlessly skeptical *Life of Jesus* gives as much as it takes away: its repudiation of the myths and legends of the Gospels pays scrupulous tribute to the authenticity of Jesus' life in its smallest details, a life that justifies Strauss's exhaustive biography. Such reverential literary biographies as Elizabeth Gaskell's *The Life of Charlotte Brontë* and John Forster's *The Life of Charles Dickens* are constructed on the same sacramental model, magnifying their subjects, as we shall see, through the same treatment Strauss gives his Christ: the "miracles" of their books matter less than the sufferings and conquests that aggrandize their experience.

In the same spirit, when George Eliot evolves from translator to creator of mighty lives, she gives us an Adam Bede who, unlike the first Adam, names nothing and does nothing, towering over his novel despite his passive role and self-righteous misjudgments; a Dorothea Brooke who is grand precisely because she is "a Saint Theresa, foundress of nothing, whose loving heart-beats and sobs after an unattained goodness tremble off and are dispersed among hindrances, instead of centering in some long-recognisable deed";[5] a Daniel Deronda who, unlike the biblical Daniel, blunders when he reads dreams, sees only vicarious visions, and ends, like Dorothea, founder of nothing. The seeming passivity of Victorian heroes, from Carlyle's Shakespeare to Eliot's Deronda, augments the authority of their lives *as* lives rather than as settings for "long-recognisable" deeds. They do nothing; they are all.

So, at least, hero-manufacturing Victorians hoped, but lives themselves might lie. To guarantee the integrity of heroes, Carlyle and his fellow prophets enclosed them in a mystic privacy not unlike that of the good women men created to feed their reverence. Activity faded into sincerity. Carlyle praises his pagan-heroes not for their deeds, but for their semisubmergence in "Nature's own laws," which are "conformable to all Truths whatsoever." This submergence in the source of truth is sincerity: "The essence of the Scandinavian, as indeed of all Pagan Mythologies, we found to be recognition of the divineness of Nature; sincere communion of man with the mysterious invisible Powers visibly seen at work in the world round him . . . Superior sincerity (far superior) consoles us for the total want of old Grecian grace. Sincerity, I think, is better than grace" (*HHW*, p. 267).

Just as Shakespeare's silence is better than speech, so sincerity (communion with invisible forces) is better than the (nontheological) grace of visible activity. Sincerity is not gregarious; it is the hidden connection of the self to powers that authenticate it, making it a repository of supraindividual truths. But the "sincerity" born of secrecy, of mystic silences, invisible communings, is the enemy of the social world. The Shakespeare who burrows

unknowably in earth's bosom exudes a sanctity immune to theatricality.

> Others abide our question. Thou art free.
> We ask and ask—Thou smilest and art still,
> Out-topping knowledge. For the loftiest hill,
> Who to the stars uncrowns his majesty,
> Planting his steadfast footsteps in the sea,
> Making the heaven of heavens his dwelling-place,
> Spares but the cloudy border of his base
> To the foiled searching of mortality;
> And thou, who didst the stars and sunbeams know,
> Self-schooled, self-scanned, self-honored, self-secure,
> Didst tread on earth unguessed at.—Better so!
> All pains the immortal spirit must endure,
> All weakness which impairs, all griefs which bow,
> Find their sole speech in that victorious brow.
>
> (Matthew Arnold, "Shakespeare," 1849)

Matthew Arnold's mountainous Shakespeare is more endear-
ing than Carlyle's suffering tree, but his essence is the same: he is
not a social being, but a natural force, knowing the stars and
sunbeams because he is like them. Insofar as he is a man, he is a
voiceless one: only his brow speaks, and only, we assume, pictorially. Arnold's final couplet asserts that Shakespeare's isolation
from humanity mystically makes him the human epitome, but
the sonnet knows only his isolation. We cannot imagine either
Carlyle's Shakespeare or Arnold's talking, much less writing dia-
logue, or going anywhere, much less putting a girdle 'round the
earth in forty minutes. Shakespeare's distinctiveness as a playwright is his versatility—he can talk like anyone we can imagine—while this heroic Shakespeare is a self-communing mono-
lith.

More mass than man, this looming entity appealed not only to
patriarchal men; his attraction was not limited to literary sages

who mistrusted the theater. The great Shakespearean actress Ellen Terry, who had no reverence for official pious frauds, wrote tenderly of Shakespeare's unwavering support for the faltering self: "My friend, my sorrow's cure, my teacher, my companion, the very eyes of me."[6] Like Carlyle's and Arnold's, Ellen Terry's Shakespeare is a fixed point in a world of distractions. He never lies, never lures us into playing with shadows, spirits, or dreams.

The nineteenth-century Shakespeare came to stand for human inviolateness, not for poetry or the theater. The Victorian mission to redeem him from theatricality is part of a cultural passion to preserve all lives from their inherently deceitful potential. It is scarcely possible to be ourselves without acting ourselves, but to be sincere, we must not act. Matthew Arnold's "The Buried Life" (1852) is a plaintive tribute to a "genuine self" driven underground by the "capricious play" that is ordinary existence:

> Fate, which foresaw
> How frivolous a baby man would be—
> By what distractions he would be possessed,
> How he would pour himself in every strife,
> And well-nigh change his own identity—
> That it might keep from his capricious play
> His genuine self, and force him to obey
> Even in his own despite his being's law,
> Bade through the deep recesses of our breast
> The unregarded river of our life
> Pursue with indiscernible flow its way.
>
> (ll. 30–40)

Like the best self, that elusive product of his ideal of Culture, Arnold's "unregarded" buried life is forced to become "indiscernible" by the variety and changes of human activity.

The theater, that alluring pariah within Victorian culture, came to stand for all the dangerous potential of theatricality to invade the authenticity of the best self. The forbidden, theatrical Shakespeare wrote that even a respectable man plays, in his lifetime, many parts. More subversively still, the inveterate actor Oscar Wilde claimed—through his fittingly corrupt mouthpiece Dorian Gray—that the sincerity Carlyle exalted is itself self-betrayal:

> Is insincerity such a terrible thing? I think not. It is merely a method by which we can multiply our personalities.
>     Such, at any rate, was Dorian Gray's opinion. He used to wonder at that shallow psychology of those who conceived the Ego in man as a thing, simple, permanent, reliable, and of one essence. To him, man was a being with myriad lives and myriad sensations, a complex multiform creature that bore within itself strange legacies of thought and passion, and whose very flesh was tainted with the monstrous maladies of the dead. [7]

Even to Wilde at his most provocative, though, this "complex multiform creature" must smell of the crypt. Wilde's impertinent tributes to insincerity rarely abandon completely Arnoldian dreams of a buried life: the being who abandons sincerity for multiplicity, self-communion for self-creation, is lurid, perverse, a ghoul. Dorian Gray's wicked reversals segregate the theatrical from the natural as sternly as do Carlyle's righteous prophecies.

## Theatrical Lives

In the theater Oscar Wilde is the most companionably giddy of playwrights, but in humanist circles the theatricality he finds at the heart of social life is synonymous with perversity and joylessness: it is a curse, not a boon, to multiply our personalities. Like their Victorian ancestors, twentieth-century sages want to believe in a self "simple, permanent, reliable, and of one essence." When it appeared in 1959 Erving Goffman's *The Presentation of Self in Everyday Life* caused something of a sensation with its Shakespearean assertion that we perform our lives as roles society assigns us. But even Goffman imagines a single, if depressed, self behind the forced impersonations, "a solitary player involved in a harried concern for his production. Behind many masks and many characters, each performer tends to wear a single look, a naked unsocialized look, a look of concentration, a look of one who is privately engaged in a difficult, treacherous task."[8]

Performing is not, for Goffman, the release of multiple selves, but a grim capitulation to social control. His favorite examples of everyday actors are citizens in servitude—women, waiters, and servants—who can control others only by becoming what is wanted. He does not say, with Dorian Gray, that acting is ghoulish, but, as in Wilde's novel, it is clearly the activity of the damned: here the damned are the powerless, those lowly enough to need to win. By implication Goffman suggests, like Carlyle, that heroes would not have to act at all.

*The Picture of Dorian Gray* represents actors as damned because they are too powerful. The naive genius Sibyl Vane commits her most efficacious suicide when she relinquishes her many selves by falling in love and into sincerity, while Dorian becomes darkly powerful by splitting himself into a hellish "sincere" portrait and an unsullied self-impersonation. *The Presentation of Self in Everyday Life* damns performers because they are servants, acting out our own damned need to become what others demand. But both imagine a theater insidiously extending itself into society and then into the dearest privacy of the mind, invalidating lives that look like models of authenticity. Lionel Trilling rarely discusses the theater directly, but he is the most uncompromising exponent of this view of a theatricality that is the enemy of humanist faith. His final, elegantly anguished book contemplates the encroachment of theatricality on that monument to truth, fiction itself.

*Sincerity and Authenticity* expresses and evades a fear that is no less a part of our Victorian legacy than Trilling's earlier humanistic invocations to transcendence, largeness and cogency. Speaking of Jane Austen, who generally reassures him, Trilling asks abruptly "whether the genre of the novel does in fact inculcate and sustain the autonomy of the self or whether it perhaps does just the opposite, leading the self into factitiousness."[9]

If art leads the self into "factitiousness" after all, nothing, in Trilling's universe, deserves to be true. *Sincerity and Authenticity* continually and compulsively assaults theatricality and role-playing in life and art on behalf of what it calls "the insistent claims of the own self" (p. 10). Its rejection of play conveys the fear that lives have nothing in them but what we see. Thus there is nothing hidden for art to touch; a noble calling shrivels into impersonation.

The "own self" is as fragile an object of belief as the inspiring advice by Polonius ("to thine own self be true") from which it derives. Fidelity to one's "own self" mocks a *Hamlet* playacted from its murky, deceiving beginning. Trilling's fear for the "own self" may be the end of a humanist faith that was always fragile, but if, in this last, beleaguered book, his sense of salvation is as insecure as Hamlet's (there is an underlying apprehension in *Sincerity and Authenticity* that we may have invented the own self only to watch its continual destruction), his sense of damnation is as firm as Wilde's: an insincere art is a demonic art because, like possession, it robs us of that own self that is our best and only self.

Jonas Barish's sobering anatomy of the persistence of anti-theatricality in Western thought places Trilling's malaise in broad cultural perspective. Barish defines, from the standpoint of a believer in the own self that is also the soul, the ontological danger of believing others' performances, whether they are literary, theatrical, or heroic: "For when a player has given over his consciousness to some form of identification with a character, or when a spectator, identifying with that character, has done the same, what happens to his own self? Is it suspended somehow for the duration of performance? And if so, is this not a spiritually dangerous state of affairs? Does it not in fact resemble demonic possession?"[10] Transfigured by hero worship into vessels of salvation, but dangerously close to theatrical creations, performers—whether they are Carlylean heroes, political dignitaries, or professional actors made up to recite words not their own—require only a shift of perspective to become devourers of the self they are supposed to heal.

Once they begin to move and play, those grandly immobile heroes erected by Victorian sages for our worship become dangerous. Freed from monolithic imagery—Carlyle's Shakespearean oak tree, Arnold's Shakespearean mountain—they forfeit the connection to nature that gives them sincerity, aligning themselves instead with the forces that destroy that center of natural and cultural coherence, the own self.

Perhaps, as Terry Castle among others has suggested, this demonic, elusive spirit of performance—with its potentially infinite denials of the ontological fixities that codify culture—is female by definition.[11] It is no accident that all the writers I quote here are men, all of whom cling to an idea of a self that is not only supremely knowable, but a supremely reassuring object of faith. As dynamic outsiders, women have always had the outsider's power, so it is tempting to personify as female the theatricality that is my subject. As Victorian authors, though, women are closer to men than this polarization makes them appear. Charlotte Brontë is as hopelessly eager as Dickens to find spiritual authority in the revelations of a life. We shall notice the many provocative ways in which women are written *about* differently from men, but they *write* as members of a common culture, willing themselves to believe in often incredible lives.

THEATRICALITY WAS NOT ONLY a spirit of Victorian culture; it was a cultural fact. The idea of the theater troubled the attempts of writers to create, in the absence of orthodox faith, a humanist religion, but most Victorian writers would not have written the works we know without the theater to inspire them. Leaving aside Dickens, whose complex attraction to and rivalry with the Victorian theater is often sentimentalized, William Thackeray, Charlotte and Emily Brontë, Lewis Carroll, Robert Browning, Alfred, Lord Tennyson, Mary Braddon, Henry James, George Eliot—to name only a canonical few—wrote for the theater, longed to write for it, or, failing to achieve theatrical success, transplanted theatrical values into the works that made them famous.[12]

More wholeheartedly than literature, visual art thrived on its symbiosis with the stage. The Pre-Raphaelite and Academic paintings that were so widely disseminated as to become, for many Victorians, the prism through which they saw the world, relied on the codes of the theater, while theatrical productions gorgeously realized those same paintings.[13] The theater is a shadowy or invisible presence in most scholarly accounts of Victorian culture, but theatricality, literal as well as figurative, pervaded not only the art but the consciousness of the age that inspired our own century's struggle to be sincere and authentic.

Around 1870 the theater cast off its aura of tabooed disrepute and began to win respectability. In that year Dickens died and George Eliot was publishing such richly theatrical historical poems as "The Legend of Jubal" and "Armgart." Thus the cheap, tawdry productions Dickens caricatured somewhat vindictively in *Nicholas Nickleby* and *Great Expectations* had, on the face of it, little in common with the production, no doubt lavish and stately, for which George Eliot hoped in vain when she planned *Daniel Deronda* as a play as well as a novel. The Victorian theater's dramatic ascent out of a cultural twilight, into a high cultural centrality even Matthew Arnold might have had to acknowledge, is the most triumphant metamorphosis of a medium founded on dramatic transformations.

In 1855 the Frenchman Frances Wey described with a precision born of astonishment the Surrey pantomime *The Prince of
Pearls, or Harlequin and Jane Shore the Queen of Grapes:*

> Now and then there is a break in the farce and the spectator is
> transported to the ethereal regions of unreality—where fairies and
> genii float in landscapes of gold, crystal and diamonds. And so
> one moves alternately from dreams of bliss to the horror of night-
> mares. But that is not all. Each one of these historical impersona-
> tions plays a dual rôle; so that at a given moment the most unex-
> pected transformations take place. Conquerors and conquered,
> executioners and victims cast off their dramatic garb and take part
> in a dishevelled Bacchanalia. The plaintive Jane Shore is now
> Columbine, Richard III a clown, Hastings Harlequin, and the
> murdered princes pantaloons. . . . Suddenly the scene changes to
> a market-place and is swarming with live chickens, turkeys, pi-
> geons, ducks. [14]

The metamorphic abundance of pantomime is the seductive essence of Victorian theatricality. Dickens wrote in his essay "A
Christmas Tree" about the utter fluidity of pantomime's effect,
"when Everything is capable, with the greatest ease, of being
changed into Anything; and 'Nothing is, but thinking makes it
so.' "[15]

Cross-dressing compounded this medley of identities. In the
course of the nineteenth century, strapping actresses took over
the role of Principal Boy, while male actors played the unsympa-
thetic female Dame. In a world where gender was malleable,
where history mutated with no transition into myth, where human pageants gave way to a fantasia of animals, "dreams of bliss"
were surely indistinguishable from "the horror of nightmares."
Paradise and terror were dangerously akin in this form whose popular climax was a transformation scene.

Transformation scenes are victories of mutability over the
Nature-revering stillness of sincerity. In as breathtaking a setting
as the company can afford, the triumphant lovers assume—or, at
times, cast off—their Harlequinade identities to celebrate all the

forms of life managerial ingenuity can invent. The famous transformation scene of Planché's extravaganza, *The Island of Jewels*
(1849), involved the metamorphosis of a vast, gilded palm tree
into a group of fairies supporting a coronet of jewels. In Carlyle's
*Heroes and Hero Worship* nature consecrates Shakespeare's stability by virtually turning him into an oak tree, but Planché's tree
can become anything: like a theater that releases us from integrity, it only plays its nature.

The respectable theater that began to take shape after midcen-
tury suppressed much of this metamorphic play; it simulated instead the more rigid identities endorsed by the society that sup-
ported it. An increasingly moralized pantomime was relegated to
children's Christmas entertainment; the predictable appearance
of its familial jollity defused its subversive allure. As time went
on, it forfeited surprises as well. Prettified spectacle, spiced by
familiar music-hall idioms, replaced surreal quirkiness. In the
decade in which the theater consolidated its new acceptability,
pantomime, in the opinion of some connoisseurs, lost its spirit:
"Hitherto the authors took in a wide field for their subjects and
invented strange stories for them, but round about the seventies
pantomimes began to restrict itself [sic] to the exposition of a few
favourite fairy tales and nursery stories such as *Cinderella, Dick
Whittington, Jack and the Beanstalk, Aladdin, Robinson Crusoe*
and so on."[16] To make itself agreeable in an age that shunned
astonishing changes, pantomime began to tell the old safe stories
over and over in the old way.

Moreover, in the melodramas that dominated the theater
throughout the century, characterization was woven out of a
complex but infallibly readable system of coded gestures: metamorphic fluidity was redeemed by a ballast of character so legible
that it verged on caricature even in its time. In H. J. Byron's popular *The Lancashire Lass; or, Tempted, Tried and True* (1867), an
apparently enigmatic character declares herself in pantomimic
codes:

REDBURN: There's sometimes a flash in your dark eyes, and a quiver of the lip, to say nothing of a grasping action of the fingers that makes me uncomfortable. I only notice it when I mention Mr. Clayton. (KATE starts. She twitches her fingers and bites her lips.) Ah, there it is again . . .

KATE: I was a forward, obstinate, self-willed girl from the first; always passionate and ungovernable.[17]

Kate's words tell us only what her finger-twitching and lip-biting have already announced. Like one of Freud's female patients, she may think she has a secret, but her body cries out the one truth that constitutes her character.

Michael R. Booth analyzes the rigidity, not only of melodramatic character, but of the melodramatic form that seems so richly varied:

The main features of melodrama are familiar: the concentration on externals, the emphasis on situation at the expense of motivation and characterization, the firm moral distinctions, the unchanging character stereotypes of hero, heroine, villain, comic man, comic woman, and good old man, physical sensation, spectacular effects (made possible by improvements in stage technology), marked musical accompaniment, the rewarding of virtue and punishing of vice, the rapid alteration between extremes of violence, pathos, and low comedy. Melodrama appears to represent a complete breakdown of dramatic forms in its variety of content; yet paradoxically it is an extremely rigid form that especially in its most popular manifestations in the working-class theatres remained fixed for a hundred years.[18]

To antitheatrical Victorians, the theater was a subversive anticulture whose illusions and seductions lured souls away; but in fact the Victorian theater shared—and eventually, self-consciously aped—the paradoxes of Victorian culture as a whole. Like Dickens' fiction, it corrected its own metamorphic vitality by specializing in characters so relentlessly, uniformly typed that their presence repudiates the transformations that swarm around them. Apparently a freeing, frightening world apart, the theater mirrored the society that alternately ostracized and adored it.

## Private Theatricals

When, in *Jane Eyre*, Rochester conquers distance and plausibility by calling "Jane! Jane! Jane!" to summon his beloved, who is miles away, he arouses the reader's own suppressed powers along with Jane's. His call has the catalyzing appeal of fiction itself: when we hear it, we, like Jane, recall ourselves, refusing treacherous alliances that look like virtue, escaping sacrifices we are expected to make. When, in *Great Expectations*, a loving convict buries Pip in privileges, requiring in exchange only that the boy keep his name, he demands of Pip what Dickens' novel demands of us: not to lose ourselves—"our own selves," as Trilling calls us—in our roles. Jane and Pip, those reiterated monosyllabic names, gather the incantatory power to persuade us as we read that we are one potent being, that our self is a soul. Victorian novels touch us when they touch the self we associate with truth: our own undivided, talismanic "Jane" or "Pip."

Often, to authenticate its reality, fiction, like actors, took the shapes of men and women: it became Pendennis, Mary Barton, David Copperfield, Romola, Mariana, Andrea del Sarto. Its province was lives; its material was those points in the life cycle where the self grows into its identity, shaping potentially dangerous volatility into uniform integrity. Childhood, conversion into maturity, and death: these are the points where the self assumes its sacred nature. Or so novelists hoped. Each of these three phases appears to be universal in its significance, but through each there dances the shadow of a performer, hinting that it could very well make up as something else.

Most of this book will explore childhood, conversion into maturity, and death as novels represent them, but two heroic biographies of novelists—Elizabeth Gaskell's *The Life of Charlotte*

*Brontë* and John Forster's *The Life of Charles Dickens*—exemplify the paradigms of development that may be articles of faith or theatrical tricks. Gaskell's *Charlotte Brontë* and Forster's *Dickens* exemplify as well the myths of gender that shape lives into exemplary patterns. Sometimes Charlotte Brontë is consummately womanly and Dickens, nobly manly, but sometimes they subvert these apparently absolute identities, in tribute perhaps to the theatricality that fascinated them both.

There are ghosts in this story as well. Victorian literature proclaims, with John Henry Newman, "I must show what I am, that it may be seen what I am not, and that the phantom may be extinguished which gibbers instead of me." Ghosts stand in a tantalizing relation to the ideal of the own self: they are the deceiving scene-stealing phantoms Newman tries to exorcise, but they are also, as we shall see, manifestations of grandeur and supreme authority. Their intrusive visits announce all the unnerving, undefinable transformations of which Victorian theatricality is capable.

Nineteenth-century ghosts are adepts at performing their identities: the phantasmagorias or "ghost-shows" of the early nineteenth century, magic-lantern displays representing specters as darting spectacles of pure illumination,[19] become at the end of the century such self-displaying apparitions as Oscar Wilde's Canterville Ghost (1887), an ancient ham who howls and gibbers mechanically through such roles as "Dumb Daniel, or the Suicide's Skeleton" or "The Vampire Monk, or the Bloodless Benedictine." If ghosts are actors, actors are regularly represented as specters, emanations, doppelgänger, apparitions, of the natural self. Actors and ghosts both appear as unnatural impositions on authentic being. But underneath their assurance that they know who they are, Victorian humanists fear that the disobedient energies of the actor and the ghost manifest truer, if trickier, "own selves" than the authorized cycle of life accommodates.

# · CHAPTER I ·

## *Little Actors*

## Fictions

Children in Victorian novels are illuminated presences because they die so often. Dying is what they do best; often, they are expected to die even when they don't. They inherit their strange holiness from Wordsworthian children, but the boys and girls Wordsworth exalts rejoice in a visionary vitality potent enough to move heaven to earth; they fortify the diminished poet by arousing his memory. Characteristic Victorian children cannot rejoice. Their main distinction is a responsiveness to death that saves them from open-endedness, turning their beginnings into endings. Their truncated lives are the unbroken, self-complete, perfectly symmetrical circles of eternity. Children on the edge of death have no time to forfeit their best selves.

They do their best to take the adult reader with them when they die; their novels become their effigies, conserving an onto-logical purity ratified by death. Weeping over the deathbeds of fictional children encourages the contaminated adult to engorge those charmed selfhoods. Only through that ritual of undiluted faith, a child's death, can Ellen Wood's *East Lynne,* one of the most popular novels of the nineteenth or any century, resolve its snarl of deceptive relationships and ambiguous identities: "The time was at hand, and the boy was quite reconciled to his fate. Merciful indeed is God to dying children! It is astonishing how very readily, where the right means are taken, they may be brought to look with pleasure, rather than fear, upon their un-known journey."[1]

Little Willie Carlyle does die with pleasure, certain that in heaven he will meet his real mother, "mamma that was," whom he scarcely remembers: Isabel Vane Carlyle has committed, in the novel's terms, the cardinal sin of deserting her family to run off with a lover. When the caddish lover deserts her and her stricken family assumes she is dead, she creeps back to East Lynne disguised as governess to her own children. Having played the lady of the house, she becomes the weeping spectator of her husband's bliss in his second marriage.

Isabel is able to change her identity so radically because grief has aged her prematurely; moreover, her face has been scarred in the train wreck in which she is supposed to have died; above all, when she loses the role of wife, she is transformed in her essence. It is no wonder that her pure son fails to recognize her in the governess who ushers him into death: his single-minded faith cannot penetrate her tangle of disguises and ambiguous selves. Little Willie's inability to know his mother indicts the secret selves of all adults.

For by the time her boy's death dissipates the novel's domestic secrets, Isabel Vane has assumed so many identities that she no longer knows who she is. Playing Mrs. Carlyle, she is the irreproachable "lady—wife—mother" to whom Ellen Wood directs her cautionary moral. But when she falls, Isabel abandons the treble fortress of this identity to become a mistress. When her death is falsely announced, she becomes legally—and symbolically as well, since she has died to everything she was—a corpse. Finally, scarred unrecognizably, she mutates from Isabel Vane to Madame Vine. As she passes from wife to servant, her life smashes into a medley of selves.

Victorian readers were lost in tears when her sickly son babbled about "angels" and "mamma" without recognizing her; they wept at the thought of their own potential unrecognizability to the uncontaminated, single-selved "I." Dying little Willie, believing in his mamma in heaven but unable to identify her on earth, became a paradigm of the authenticity of all dying children,

while his metamorphosing mother became the star of the most
popular play of its time. The best-known and most reliably tear-
inducing line in the dramatization was Lady Isabel's despairing:
"Oh, Willie, my child dead, dead, dead! and he never knew me,
never called me Mother!"[2] The dying child repudiates the lie of
others' lives, embodying instead our lost original perfection.

The theater, though, threatened to undermine even that serene arbiter of being. Despite the importance of his gender in the
novel (as the oldest boy and his father's namesake, he is the heir
of all the patriarchal virtues and privileges *East Lynne* exhorts us
to venerate), onstage Willie was generally played by a girl. The
stage little Willie threatens to become a mutable being like his
mother, his inviolate identity dissipating into a play of roles.
Thus in the theater his integrity needed cosmic ratification: the
popular concluding tableau of Willie and Lady Isabel sitting bliss-
fully in Heaven on a cloud guaranteed his death the spiritual authority it has by definition in the novel.

*East Lynne* pays a crescendo of reverence to an inspired presence that passes through innumerable Victorian novels. *Jane
Eyre's* saintly consumptive Helen Burns is similarly authorizing.
When Jane, the soul of truth, is persecuted as a liar by hypocriti-
cal Mr. Brocklehurst, Helen restores her pride: "just as they all
rose, stifling my breath and constricting my throat, a girl came up
and passed me: in passing, she lifted her eyes. What a strange
light inspired them! What an extraordinary sensation that ray
sent through me! It was as if a martyr, a hero, had passed a slave
or victim, and imparted strength in the transit. I mastered the
rising hysteria, lifted up my head, and took a firm stand on the
stool."[3] That archetype of the moribund child, Dickens' Little
Nell, does not inspire rebellion, but she does, like Willie Carlyle
and Helen Burns, elicit the best selves of others:

> The people of the village, too, of whom there was not one but
> grew to have a fondness for poor Nell; even among them, there
> was the same feeling; a tenderness towards her—a compassionate

regard for her, increasing every day. The very schoolboys, light-hearted and thoughtless as they were, even they cared for her. The roughest among them was sorry if he missed her in the usual place upon his way to school, and would turn out of the path to ask for her at the latticed window. If she were sitting in the church, they perhaps might peep in softly at the open door; but they never spoke to her, unless she rose and went to speak to them. Some feeling was abroad which raised the child above them all.[4]

These three representative children become touchstones as authoritative as Matthew Arnold's inviolate ideal of poetry: they banish false selves and restore best selves. These strangely seductive dying children bathe us in the reproachful, impersonal purity of our birthright. Victorian children are always about to disappear, taking with them the integrity of the weeping, believing reader.

Their admonitory, evaporating presences are most perfectly realized as ghosts; in a sense, the integrated self they represent is always a ghost among the colorful confusions of life. In *Wuthering Heights* the child-ghost of Catherine cuts through tangles of adult identities in the manner of *East Lynne*'s dying little Willie, though here the chaos of identities the child-ghost resolves is that of her own adult self. The adult Catherine has no self. As a young woman, she proclaims grandly but falsely, "I *am* Heathcliff," but she signs her window ledge as a medley of Catherines: "This writing, however, was nothing but a name repeated in all kinds of characters, large and small—*Catherine Earnshaw;* here and there varied to *Catherine Heathcliff,* and then again to *Catherine Linton.*"[5] The ghost is only "Catherine Linton"; she integrates the fractured being of the wife into the outcast integrity of the child. Alive, Catherine is everyone and no one; the child-ghost is her restored self.

Rudyard Kipling's story " 'They' " (1904) is the eerie essence of this charismatic union of childhood and death. In " 'They,' a child-loving narrator becomes captivated by a tender blind woman, who is herself enthralled by a swarm of seductive children; we learn at the end that these children are tantalizing ghosts who have returned from heaven. They exist only as elusive chortles, rustles, and shadows, but they are the most vivid presences in the story; the adults who half-perceive them have no lives beyond that of hierophants, waiting for mystic manifestations of the dead. Kipling makes available no other religion; no living child, we feel, could be as spiritually significant as these playful revenants.

WHEN CHILDREN IN NOVELS do not die, they realize their beings in terror: dying children offer revelations growing ones resist. In two well-known moments of harrowing self-discovery, Charlotte Brontë's Jane Eyre and Charles Dickens' Pip learn who they are, teaching their readers who they too might be. Characteristically, both aggressively reject death: Jane Eyre confronts Mr. Brocklehurst, who responds only to children in heaven or hell, with her creed: "I must keep in good health and not die" (*JE*, p. 64). She does just this throughout her tale, while her intimates sicken and fall around her. Pip never makes so bald a declaration; he simply, coolly, survives numerous killers. He is neither devoured by Magwitch's cannibalistic young man nor hanged with George Barnwell nor consumed in the fire that ignites Miss Havisham nor dissolved in Orlick's limekiln nor drowned with Compeyson. Both Jane and Pip fight to preserve themselves, but, characteristically, the girl confronts that self in prison, while the boy does so shivering at the expanding enormity of the world.

Jane Eyre's prison begins in a room, but swells into the awful enclosure of her own angry self. In one of the great Victorian evocations of fear, a little girl looks in a mirror:

Alas, yes [they had locked the door]! no jail was ever more secure. Returning, I had to cross before the looking-glass; my fascinated glance involuntarily explored the depth it revealed. All looked colder and darker in that visionary hollow than in reality: and the strange little figure there gazing at me with a white face and arms specking the gloom, and glittering eyes of fear moving where all else was still, had the effect of a real spirit: I thought it like one of the tiny phantoms, half fairy, half imp (*JE*, p. 46).

A later, more apparently docile little girl, Lewis Carroll's Alice, has the same vertigo when, in *Through the Looking-Glass,* a text more explicitly fantastic than *Jane Eyre,* her mirror becomes "a sort of mist" and she descends into a room "as different as possible" from her familiar one, in which she herself is invisible. In both, a little girl finds herself as an alien creature; in both, the depth of the looking glass evokes analogous depths in the little girl's own nature. The fascination of the looking glass welds the domestic to the strange: the little girl apprehends in it both her own "glittering eyes of fear" and the new, superimposed life of "a real spirit." Becoming the eerie figure she sees properly for the first time, Jane Eyre falls into a fit of terror at the realization of her powers.

Jane's vision of her own unrealized depths has the magnitude of a parable: the child who will not cherish her supreme self by dying is stricken by her capacity in a flash of sacred terror. The meaning of this moment is "the depth it reveals." When Jane Eyre looks at herself, she recovers for her readers the magic within their masks of normalcy.

Pip, in *Great Expectations,* is terrified, not by the depths within him but by the unboundedness without. He learns himself, not through imprisonment but in the featureless graves of his parents and the wasteland surrounding those graves; his revelation is punctuated only by bleak "beyond"s. Realizing himself, he learns "that the dark flat wilderness beyond the churchyard, intersected with dykes and mounds and gates, with scattered cattle feeding on it, was the marshes; and that the low leaden line beyond, was the river; and that the distant savage lair from which the wind was rushing, was the sea; and that the small bundle of shivers growing afraid of it all and beginning to cry, was Pip."[6]

Pip's initiation is as momentous as Jane's. It has, like hers, a parable's universal resonance: consciousness is born in bleakness and learns its nature—in Pip's case, its capacity for fear—from vastness. Pip's talismanic word, however, is not "the depths," but "beyond." He learns the lesson of all heroic men, that his being is important because it is the only life in receding empty spaces. Jane Eyre falls into her self-awareness; Pip expands into his.

The difference between the children's discoveries is in part a difference of gender. When readers take Jane Eyre and Pip into themselves, making the characters' lives epitomes of their own, they are learning the depths and the waste spaces of their own identities as men and women. It is the nature of the girl to fall through her looking glass into selfhood; Lewis Carroll's Alice does so as readily as Jane Eyre, becoming a queen through this fall, as does Jane in her own stern way. It is the nature of the boy to diffuse himself into the horror of space; Stevenson's Jim Hawkins becomes a self on the sea, Kipling's Kim in a boundless India that is full of treacherous secrets. The girl's claustrophobia modulates into the boy's agoraphobia. The terrors of self-discovery include the suggestion that gender is as absolute as being itself.

The quest for the own self that motivates Victorian literature of development encourages readers to imagine glory at the end, but this self is never cozy. When the novel assumes a child's voice, it lures us into believing that that child is ourselves as we really are. Whether that child dies to preserve itself or learns itself in terror, its ceremonial departures and discoveries guide us into our own rebirth. The two famous children who since their births have wielded magnetic power over readers' identities—Jane Eyre and Pip—announce that the child is not only the incarnation of inviolate being: it flowers into being according to the rules and taboos of its gender.

Twentieth-century accounts of the bildungsroman reinforce this definition of a genre identifying children's beings with nature and nature with immutable divisions of gender: critics freely use boys and girls to authenticate the separations between men and women. Jerome Hamilton Buckley, for instance, defines a largely male tradition whose essential pattern is the expansion that brings Pip haunted self-realization—his typical protagonist moves outward through "childhood, the conflict of generations, provinciality, the larger society, self-education, alienation, ordeal by love, the search for a vocation and a working philosophy"— while a recent account of the female bildungsroman is restrictively titled *The Voyage In.*[7] Yet if we look only at divisive gender stereotypes, we will miss the communality of the myths that give Victorian novels their power.

Even a novel like George Eliot's *The Mill on the Floss,* which seems utterly reliant on mutually exclusive male and female paradigms, defines these paradigms only to undermine them. Tom and Maggie Tulliver are rent by an ontological distance that seems similar to the division between Jane Eyre's ceremonial initiation and Pip's, but the novel's strength lies in its subtle distinctions. Like Jane, "loving, large-souled Maggie" commands "the depths in life," finding her powers in a spot fittingly called "the Red Deeps." The medium of her self-discovery is not a humble looking glass, but a larger mirror of her unruly soul, the turbulent river Floss.

Tom's destiny, like Pip's, lies in the expansion his father forces on him. "I don't *mean* Tom to be a miller and farmer. I see no fun i' that: why, if I made him a miller an' farmer, he'd be expectin' to take to the mill an' the land, an' a-hinting at me as it was time for me to lay by an' think of my latter end. . . . I shall give Tom an eddication an' put him to a business, as he may make a nest for himself an' not want to push me out o' mine."[8] Tom acquires the ruthlessness his father expects: the inhumanity of his honor makes him another order of being from the sister who sees only the enormity of the personal.

*The Mill on the Floss* is a wonderful novel not because it adheres to this rigid scheme, but because it subverts it. For one thing, before both siblings evade their destinies by dying, their father's bankruptcy forces them out of their prescribed lives. Tom must after all return home and take over Mr. Tulliver's nest by redeeming his debts, while Maggie is forced to leave the home that fed her insistent interiority. Destinies, the novel suggests, are contingent on economics, not on gender divisions rooted in nature. Moreover, the natures of Tom and Maggie fail to fit prescribed Victorian patterns. In his obsession with honor, Tom Tulliver is closer in nature to Charlotte Brontë's iron-willed Jane Eyre than he is to Pip; Dickens' hero, like Maggie Tulliver, knows only love or its absence. In the myths these novels compose, boys and girls are fluid; rhetoric, not nature, separates them. The iconography with which boys are represented is uniform, however, and girls do not share it. No matter who they are, girls find their lives in "the depths," while boys discover themselves "beyond."

On the face of it, the sacred power of the child appropriates the authority of nature to immunize the sexes from each other. The probity of the child's nature, the authority of children over our own natures, is a peculiarly Victorian myth that Victorian literature both clings to and resists. This reliance on childhood for answers about ourselves is not universal; it wanes in certain ages. At the beginning of the rebellious decade of the 1960s Philippe Ariès wrote wittily, if prematurely: "It is as if, to every period of history, there corresponded a privileged age and a particular division of human life: 'youth' is the privileged age of the seventeenth century, childhood of the nineteenth, adolescence of the twentieth."[9] But politics and ideologies determine our "privileged age": an audience as unnerved by its own potential instability as the Victorian middle class rejects the volatile adolescent as its conduit into selfhood, turning to children's apparent immutability, just as the conservative, authority-loving decade of the 1980s has done.[10]

DIFFERENCES ARE EASY to magnify, but it is the commonality between Pip and Jane Eyre that remains enthralling: at the beginning of their stories both children are flung upon the enormity of the fact that they are who they are. Their baptisms remain both appealing and chilling. They appeal because, although Jane and Pip are children, they are not cute and their natures are not small: their self-realization is a consecration into mightiness. But the magnitude of their revelations is unnerving because a taunt is hidden in their mighty claims: if Jane is a tiny phantom with the mask of a child, and Pip a juvenile pretender, what becomes of their mighty self-awareness—and of our own?

At first, Jane Eyre, imprisoned in a dead man's room, and Pip in a waste of graves and empty places appear compellingly integrated. They share the epic self-consciousness of Carlyle's sage Diogenes Teufelsdröckh when, in *Sartor Resartus*, he learns that he is not his parents' child: "A certain poetic elevation, yet also a corresponding civic depression, it naturally imparted: *I was like no other*; in which fixed-idea, leading sometimes to highest, and oftener to frightfullest results, may there not lie the first spring of Tendencies, which in my Life have become remarkable enough? . . . my fellows are perhaps not numerous."[11]

Carlyle was his century's arbiter of grandeur; his heroes provided patterns of sacred lives. Teufelsdröckh's awe at the fearful capacity of his remarkableness set the tone for the self-confrontations of his age. But when our intimately known fictional children mimic Teufelsdröckh's exaltation, the ceremony changes subtly: Teufelsdröckh exalts himself through his voice, clothing his reflections in an elaborately mannered, metaphorical language that displays the magnificence of his subject, while Jane and Pip see themselves as spectacles.

In the revelations that begin *Great Expectations* and *Jane Eyre* the narrative emphasis is on the scene and what is seen: Jane and Pip's selves appear to them from without, like the child-ghosts in *Wuthering Heights* or "'They.'" In each case the apparition is a visually compelling alien to the teller of the tale, who functions, with the reader, as audience of the vision. Jane Eyre sees herself as "one of the tiny phantoms, half fairy, half imp," who peopled not only Victorian children's lore, but also theatrical pantomimes. Teufelsdröckh's pronouncement "*I was like no other*" breaks into an "I" that is haunted by an other. The Jane in the mirror seems in every sense of the word made up, eliciting not intimacy, but the fascinating distance of a play.

Pip aggrandizes himself by his vision of the landscape, but then, like Jane, he enters that scene as a distanced apparition, "the small bundle of shivers growing afraid of it all and beginning to cry." But this small Pip is not congruent with the vastness of his vision; the seen self, a figure of conventional theatrical pathos, seems an alternative to the audacity of the narrating self, not its projection. The sweeping seeing eye splits off from the dwarfed "I." The striking visual immediacy of Jane's sudden appearance as imp, Pip's as small bundle of shivers, is the essence of Victorian pictorial theater.

As in that theater, visual amazement is the heart of the scene. Living pictures were the source of Victorian theatrical excitement; like those pictures, Jane and Pip's initiations are striking in their lack of inwardness. The children require no rumination or analysis to absorb their selves; they need only see them. The moment of sight is the moment of revelation. Their self-realizations are not the explications our own post-Freudian age requires; they are the visual realizations that structured the Victorian pictorial theater.

Martin Meisel defines this complex visual interchange: "'Realization,' which had a precise technical sense when applied to certain theatrical tableaux based on well-known pictures, . . . meant both literal re-creation and translation into a more real, that is more vivid, visual, physically present medium. To move from mind's eye to body's eye was realization, and to add a third dimension to two was realization, as when words became picture, or when picture became dramatic tableaux."[12] In the pictorial theater and in the culture it taught to see, everything was visually manifest. Kate in H. J. Byron's *The Lancashire Lass* revealed herself pantomimically, as we saw, in her finger-twitching and lip-biting. In the same spirit, the most acclaimed Victorian actresses turned themselves into intricate visual semaphores: Sarah Bernhardt, Ellen Terry, and Eleonora Duse each "created her own sign conventions through which audiences perceived her."[13] To be was to be seen.

The tableaux that set off these performers were prismatic displays in which the characters watched each other, each seeing a different scene, while the audience saw all the gazes that composed the whole. C. H. Hazelwood's adaptation of Mary E. Braddon's *Aurora Floyd* (1863), for instance, ends the first act with a climactic tableau structured by the characters' dissonant looks at each other.

Braddon's novel is, like *East Lynne*, a sensation story built around the mystery of its volatile heroine's unreadable nature as it manifests itself in secret relationships. In Braddon's novel various enthralled men try to read Aurora. Onstage, they need only watch her. At the end of the first act her unscrupulous first husband, James, who is her father's former groom, returns from supposed death (as Isabel Vane does in *East Lynne*) to make Aurora, now contentedly married to John, a bigamist. Steve and Mrs. Powell, wicked servants, plot to expose her.

AURORA. . . . Come—come—don't look serious. Why don't you smile, John. Why don't you laugh, John—laugh as I do. Ha—ha—ha!

(forcing a gay laugh, which suddenly turns into an hysterical one, wild and piercing, so as to express great mental agony—this requires to be done with great force so as to achieve a climax as she falls into the arms of JOHN—at this moment MRS. POWELL appears at the window and *looks in exultingly*—STEVE points exultingly to the certificate he holds in his hand, *regarding* AURORA with *looks of hate* as he stands by door, R.—JAMES with his hands in his pockets, and one leg coolly crossed over the other, *looks on with indifference.* Tableau-Music.) (Act I, scene 3; my emphasis.)

Like that of most Victorian sensation fiction, the mystery of *Aurora Floyd* springs from unknowability of character. A seemingly transparent protagonist turns out to be many possible people, but, until the final hurried resolution, she is none of them for long. Defining herself only by her cryptic mad laugh, Aurora is the repository of others' conflicting gazes. Like the great pictorial actresses who dominated Victorian theater, she becomes the eyes who look at her.

Tom Robertson's *Caste* (1867) is ideologically opposed to *Aurora Floyd* and all sensation drama. *Caste* exemplifies the mutation of nineteenth-century drama theater historians dub the "Robertsonian Revolution," which brought muted domestic realism, and consequently respectable middle-class audiences, into the theater of the 1860s. The characters in *Caste* have little ambiguity; only their situations perplex them. Esther, the heroine, was once an actress, but we are quickly reassured that she is "an amiable, good girl." At the climax of her story she defines herself, not with a cryptic mad laugh, but definitively: "I am a woman—I am a wife—a widow—a *mother!*" Esther *is* the roles sensation drama calls into question. Accordingly, Robertson rewards her integrity by resurrecting her husband at the final curtain.

Robertson's notion of character is so solid, and, in our sense, so antitheatrical that one would not expect him to conclude *Caste* with the same sort of tableau—a symphony of gazes on which the audience gazes—that concludes the first act of *Aurora Floyd:* "ECCLES falls off the chair in the last stage of drunkenness, bottle in hand. HAWTREE, leaning one foot on chair from which ECCLES has fallen, *looks at him through eye-glass.* SAM enters, and goes to POLLY, B.C., behind cradle, and, producing wedding-ring from several papers, *holds it up before her eyes.* ESTHER plays until curtain drops."[14]

As in *Aurora Floyd,* the characters complete themselves by seeing each other and being seen; the audience blesses them by watching the composition they make. The centrality of Polly's wedding ring assures us that this web of gazes provides final definitions, not further questions. Only Esther, the piano-playing heroine, can define herself aurally: she is so fully known that no one onstage need look at her at all. The characters nevertheless live, for each other and for us, pictorially. Whether the picture provides enigmas or answers, theatrical being is being seen.

In a theater of realizations, tableaux vivants, spectacles, and surreal visual transformations, the "meaning" of a character or an action is its visual manifestation. The transformation scenes that were the climax of pantomime featured spectacular metamorphoses: the central players burst forth in transfigured *commedia dell'arte* incarnations, and, in the concluding Grand Transformation, were transported to a lavish Paradise.[15] Familiar but magically changed, the renewed identities of pantomime convention, like the enhanced eye-engorging figures of melodramatic tableaux, are more splendid, but no less dramatic, than those of Jane and Pip in their own transformation scenes. Steeped, despite themselves, in theatrical modes of breathtaking visual transformations, Jane Eyre and Pip become child-seers, not only in Carlyle's sense, but in the theater's: they realize themselves when they *see* themselves theatrically translated. The self is not, after all, a single noble entity, with the child its keeper. The self is a spectacle; the child is not its priest, but its audience and one of its masks.

THE LURE OF THE STAGE CHILD troubled child-worshipers throughout the nineteenth century. Even Wordsworth's great incantatory "Ode: Intimations of Immortality from Recollections of Early Childhood," which licensed a hundred years of acolytes to defer to the child as a "Mighty Prophet! Seer blessed! / On whom these truths do rest, / Which we are toiling all our lives to find" (ll. 114–116), contained a stanza over which few Wordsworthians lingered. In it the actor-child chafes restlessly under the burden of the seer:

> See, at his feet, some little plan or chart,
> Some fragment from his dreams of human life,
> Shaped by himself with newly-learned art;
> A wedding or a festival,
> A mourning or a funeral;
> And this hath now his heart,
> And unto this he frames his song:
> Then will he fit his tongue
> To dialogues of business, love, or strife;
> But it will not be long
> Ere this be thrown aside,
> And with new joy and pride
> The little Actor cons another part;
> Filling from time to time his "humorous stage"
> With all the Persons, down to palsied Age,
> That Life brings with her in her equipage;
> As if his whole vocation
> Were endless imitation.
>
> (ll. 91–107)

Wordsworth's dream-child may be a repository of mighty truths, but his real child spurts forth mock-selves in alarmingly agile play. When Wordsworth composed these lines in 1804, thirteen-year-old Master Betty was the sensation of London. As Hamlet, Macbeth, and other mature heroes, this weirdly charismatic boy outdrew all adult competitors, including the novice Edmund Kean, whom the Romantics were to cast as their type of genius.

In 1837, the year of Queen Victoria's accession, a restless young native of Portsmouth named Ben Terry fell in love with the stage when he saw the child actress Jean Davenport being, it seemed, all things: she danced a hornpipe, then turned into a spine-tingling Shylock, and concluded with a fantasia of male and female, juvenile and adult, roles in a piece called *The Manager's Daughter*. Terry trained his daughters Kate and Ellen to emulate Jean Davenport's versatility. A disapproving Dickens pilloried the mercurial little girl by turning her into the repulsive Infant Phenomenon in *Nicholas Nickleby*, rigidified by gin-and-water into perpetual, spurious stage innocence. Yet through her influence on Kate and Ellen Terry, Jean Davenport inspired a theatrical dynasty that still exists.[16]

Until the 1860s, when the theater began to court middle-class respectability, stage children were miracles of virtuosity, not adorableness. In the space of a performance, child stars whirled from youth to age, female to male, burlesque to tragedy, and back again. Like Wordsworth's "little Actor," they filled their stage with "all the Persons, down to palsied Age," adults become in lifetimes. Humbler working-class child supers became creatures—the imps, fairies, and elves of pantomime and extravaganza. Like the imprisoned young Jane Eyre, who in the Red Room casts off her human disguise when her preternatural self rises up in the mirror, the child-as-actor is less the origin and end of identity than a troubling kaleidoscope of beings beyond the acceptable.

## Lives

Victorian biographies build bridges between the passionate myths of fiction and the indisputable authority of fact. They generally focus, as *Sartor Resartus* does, on childhood as the holy origin of their subjects' heroism, but biographical children reveal natures still more amorphous than those of their fictional counterparts. Elizabeth Gaskell's *The Life of Charlotte Brontë* and John Forster's *The Life of Charles Dickens* make much of the scarred childhoods at the root of their subjects' genius, but the young Charlotte Brontë and Charles Dickens prove less revelatory than elusive. Like their own creations, Jane Eyre and Pip, the supposed mighty prophets on whom the truths of the self rest slide from integrity into performance of multiple, bewildering selves.

Gaskell's Charlotte Brontë is stunted by tragedy, but deprivation suits her rare nature. Her childhood is shaped by the deaths of women. Her mother dies first; her saintly older sister Maria takes charge of the family until her own death and that of the next sister, Elizabeth. These chosen children are beyond childhood. Maria bequeaths to all her sisters her transcendence of nature's cycle: "Her childhood was no childhood; the cases are rare in which the possessors of great gifts have known the blessings of that careless happy time; *their* unusual powers stir within them, and, instead of the natural life of perception,—the objective, as the Germans call it—they begin the deeper life of reflection—the subjective."[17]

Wordsworth's consecrated spirits draw their vitality from the childhood Gaskell's consecrated Brontë sisters rise above. Patterning herself after Maria, the young Charlotte Brontë is closer to eerily old stage children like Master Betty than she is to the ordinary "careless" children Gaskell dismisses; her withered youth links her to those oracular old children who visit Victorian novels, *Bleak House*'s Charley and young Smallweed, or *Jude the Obscure*'s Father Time. Children who are not children are hallowed, if dangerous, presences in the Victorian imagination. Like stage children, they are compellingly unnatural.

At the same time as Gaskell is awed by the unnaturalness of

these siblings, she asks us to mourn the "natural" childhoods of the Brontës, stunted by the violent assaults of their half-mad father. In a curiously undefined episode, Mr. Brontë places a mask over the faces of his timid children so that they will "stand and speak boldly from under the cover of the mask" (p. 94). Anticipating Oscar Wilde's exuberant defense of theatricality in "The Critic as Artist"—"Man is least himself when he talks in his own person. Give him a mask and he will tell you the truth"—Mr. Brontë ignores his century's aesthetic of nature and sincerity, leading his talented children to theatrical truths.[18]

Gaskell refrains at first from judging this unorthodox method of ascertaining "the hidden characters of his children." Only in retrospect does she condemn the distortions it imposes: "Wild, strong hearts, and powerful minds, were hidden under an enforced propriety, just as their faces had been concealed by their father, under his stiff, unchanging mask" (p. 108).

But does the father's mask conceal or reveal the buried child-natures—if indeed the Brontës were ever children? In the course of the story the privileged son collapses when he is sent to London to become a genius in his own person, but the three surviving sisters come into their powers writing pseudo-confessions pseudonymously. "Currer Bell" is as effective a mask as Jane Eyre or Lucy Snowe; both allow Charlotte Brontë to simulate a sincerity impossible in her life as Gaskell presents it. Gaskell's biography glorifies its subject by denying her a childhood, while condemning the mask her father imposes for blighting that childhood. Despite Gaskell's expressed intention, though, her story leads us to believe in "the hidden character" that "speaks boldly [only] under the cover of the mask."

Gaskell's *Life* is suggestively ambiguous regarding the source of its subject's power. It takes its tone from Mary Taylor's touching phrase, which Gaskell quotes without comment: "The whole family used to 'make out' histories, and invent characters and events. I told [Charlotte] sometimes they were like growing pota-

toes in a cellar. She said, sadly, 'Yes! I know we are!'" (p. 132).
But are the potatoes subject or object of this sentence? In other
words, are the children themselves the "growing potatoes," part
of nature if a submerged part, in danger of suffocation by unnatural isolation? Or are they the growers *of* the potatoes, the
strange dreams and fancies which would become their art? In
Mary Taylor's half-accusatory description as in Gaskell's biography, the artist children hover between potatoes and the mask, or
between nature and theater. We never know whether their books
come from the depths of the cellar or from the self-concealing,
self-creating mask their father imposes on them.

To Elizabeth Gaskell the young Charlotte Brontë is an uncomfortable anomaly, half-natural, half-fabricated, but John Forster's
authorized biography of Dickens is rooted in its subject's childhood. Forster's biographical mission (engineered by Dickens himself) is the revelation of the boy's humiliating labor in a blacking
warehouse after his father's imprisonment for debt. His publica-
tion of Dickens' autobiographical fragment, which vividly recre-
ates the exquisite suffering of a sensitive boy fallen from family,
from school, from class, from his great expectations of a triumphant future, presents a paradigm of childhood deprivation that
has "explained" Dickens from Forster's day to our own.[19] To Forster the child is the soul and source of the adult's authentic perceptions: "But my experience of him led me to put implicit faith in
the assertion he unvaryingly himself made, that he had never
seen any cause to correct or change what in his boyhood was his
own secret impression of anybody, whom he had, as a grown man,
the opportunity of testing in later years."[20] In Forster's influential
biography the child is not only father to the man: he is the true
man.

Forster's *Life of Charles Dickens* keeps faith with its subject by
preserving his voice in letters and documents; the life is unsev-
ered from its author's narrative power. Forster explains with suit-
able reverence that "the purpose here was to make Dickens the

sole central figure in the scenes revived, *narrator as well as principal actor*" (I, 377; my italics). The intimate portrait Forster's method seems to promise guarantees that his subject will retain the theatrical control he demands.

As narrator, Dickens is still more solicitous than Forster of his own importance as "principal actor." His ordeal in the blacking warehouse threatens his specialness with hateful submergence in the commonplace—"I know that I worked, from morning to night, with common men and boys, a shabby child" (I, 25)—but no shabbiness can make this resilient little performer common. He dignifies his lost self by Byronic, quasi-blasphemous imagery: "small Cain that I was, except that I had never done harm to anyone" (I, 23). Like Cain, he matters enough to be shunned by all the powers, human and divine, while remaining, like Christ, specially preserved from original sin. He is at once so bad and so good that everyone must notice him. His exquisite sufferings are authenticated less by their secrecy than by their effect on the audiences life throws in his way.

Even as a shabby laborer, pasting labels on bottles, The Inimitable finds himself in displays of skill. Along with Bob Fagin, whose name will grace Dickens' deftest showman of a villain, he shows off his dexterity at the warehouse window: "Sometimes there would be quite a little crowd there. I saw my father coming in at the door one day when we were very busy, and I wondered how he could bear it" (I, 32). He goes on to speculate that this performance of labor was so devastating to his father as to effect at last his belated rescue from the warehouse. Whether he is showing off or baring his wounds, Dickens ascribes to his public presence the power to move fate. The skillful drama of a boy's agony in a warehouse window will move the heart of a nation of fathers when, years later, the man kills little Paul Dombey over and over again on a series of stages.

Even his hours of solitary leisure are dignified by their effect on those who see him. When the forlorn child goes to a beef-house in Drury Lane (the heart of London's theatrical district), the help is insufficiently distraught at the sight of him. As Dickens recalls: "What the waiter thought of such a strange little apparition, coming in all alone, I don't know; but I can see him now, staring at me as I ate my dinner, and bringing up the other waiter to look. I gave him a halfpenny, and I wish, now, that he hadn't taken it" (I, 23). Neither the child nor the adult Dickens stops to consider that the waiter may need the halfpenny more than the "strange little apparition" who claims exclusive narrative attention. He elicits a more gratifying response from a good woman in a public house: "They served me with the ale, though I suspect it was not the strongest on the premises; and the landlord's wife, opening the little half-door and bending down, gave me a kiss that was half-admiring and half-compassionate, but all womanly and good, I am sure" (I, 29). Like an actor, the boy *is* when he makes others feel. His appearance as an "apparition," a title he regularly gives himself in the *Life,* has the power to jolt common people out of their meagerness.

The biography begins with a magic moment in which that apparition confronts a man: the successful author encounters his mystic boy self at his Gadshill home. He describes a meeting with another order of being:

> So smooth was the old high road, and so fresh were the horses, and so fast went I, that it was midway between Gravesend and Rochester, and the widening river was bearing the ships, white-sailed or black-smoked, out to sea, when I noticed by the wayside a very queer small boy.
>
> "Holloa!" said I, to the very queer small boy, "where do you live?"
>
> "At Chatham," says he.
>
> "What do you do there?" says I.
>
> "I go to school," says he.

I took him up in a moment, and we went on. Presently the very queer small boy says, "This is Gadshill we are coming to, where Falstaff went out to rob those travellers, and ran away."

"You know something about Falstaff, eh?" said I.

"All about him," said the very queer small boy. "I am old (I am nine), and I read all sorts of books. But *do* let us stop at the top of the hill, and look at the house there, if you please!"

"You admire that house?" said I.

"Bless you, sir," said the very queer small boy, "when I was not more than half as old as nine, it used to be a treat for me to be brought to look at it. And now I am nine, I come by myself to look at it. And ever since I can recollect, my father, seeing me so fond of it, has often said to me, *If you were to be very persevering, and were to work hard, you might some day come to live in it.* Though that's impossible!" said the very queer small boy, drawing a low breath, and now staring at the house out of a window with all his might.

I was rather amazed to be told this by the very queer small boy; for that house happens to be *my* house, and I have reason to believe that what he said was true. (I, 5)

This apparent union between past and present selves leads to an abyss. The very queer small boy is never permitted to share the amazed narrator's consciousness; he remains a weird visitant, despite the fact that he has given the narrator his ambition and his home. The old and the young Dickens have no more in common than Peter Pan and Wendy do; they are friendly beings of opposing species. The reader, like the artist, is bereft of an "I" to rest in.

Victorian biographies of the great and famous were intended to provide exemplars of the evolving self; the chosen child, realizing with Carlyle's Teufelsdröckh that *"I was like no other,"* provides, in theory, an orderly Wordsworthian seedbed for the noble adult who becomes a pattern for all noble adults. But in Elizabeth Gaskell's and John Forster's exemplary biographies, despite the role the careful biographer assigns it, the child splits off from its place in the cycle of growth, becoming a taunting multiselved specter, presenting itself, like a ghost, in all its ambiguous visual significance. The naturally growing self explodes into the pyrotechnical self who expels its identities into spectacle. The very queer small Dickens, the masked Charlotte Brontë, are neither father to the man nor mother to the woman. Instead of reinforcing the integrity of the adult's "own self," they decompose that self into fragments.

Victorian fiction provided a mirror—if a magic one—wherein readers could live the intensest life they were capable of. Through novels, which at heart are wishes rather than realism, they imagined themselves regaining undiluted being. Biographies provided models of development according to approved principles of self-help, encouraging readers to construct their own lives. But at the same time fiction and biography exposed to destruction the selves they exalted. One sort of book remained to restore the sore spirit to its original home: fantasy, vivid and beloved, allowed even adult readers—and perhaps especially adults—to rest in an imagined primal stability.

## Fantasies

The best-known Victorian fantasies are ostensibly written for children. Many give childhood a magic, metamorphic country, a Wonderland or a Neverland, insulating children from the adult species of which they are the supposed source or anchor. Others, especially the many ghost stories of which haunting children are the subject but not the implied audience, revel in their representations of children as remote spectral presences. This ghostliness expresses everything they are by implication in "realistic" novels and biographies. At their most intensely realized, as ghosts or mystic apparitions of a vanished personal past, children are another order of being than the adults they frighten and tantalize.

Victorian child-ghosts are not the satanic monsters on which our own Gothic literature feeds. They are something subtler, innocent, admonitory, and terrifying at the same time. In many stories they have died the victims of corrupt adults, but, as with the child-ghost of Catherine in *Wuthering Heights,* their vulnerability enhances their spectacular power. The ghost of a little boy in Charlotte Riddell's "Walnut-Tree House" has the visual charisma of Dickens' Pip, or of Dickens himself in his autobiographical fragment, but Riddell's child gains the intensified power of the dead: "For suddenly the door opened, and there entered, shyly and timidly, a little child—a child with the saddest face mortal ever beheld; a child with wistful eyes and long, ill-kept hair; a child poorly dressed, wasted and worn, and with the mournfullest expression on its countenance that face of a child ever wore."[21]

The entrance of this child is the most powerful moment in the story, just as the entrance of the ill-kept young Dickens into a public house is—or should have been—the most powerful moment in the lives of the waiters. This ghost is placated with relative ease: he recovers the little sister, now grown-up, from whom mercenary adults have separated him. Pictorial child-ghosts, like those in M. R. James's "Lost Hearts," are harder to erase. These two ghosts have lost not merely their inheritance, but their hearts, to an adult acolyte of pagan magic. They appear in the garden to warn a third potential victim:

> Whilst the girl stood still, half smiling, with her hands clasped over her heart, the boy, a thin shape, with black hair and ragged clothing, raised his arms in the air with an appearance of menace and of unappeasable hunger and longing. The moon shone upon his almost transparent hands, and Stephen saw that the nails were fearfully long and that the light shone through them. As he stood with his arms thus raised, he disclosed a terrifying spectacle. On the left side of his chest there opened a black and gaping rent; and there fell upon Stephen's brain, rather than upon his ear, the im-

pression of one of those hungry and desolate cries that he had
heard resounding over the woods of Aswarby all that evening. In
another moment this dreadful pair had moved swiftly and noise-
lessly over the dry gravel, and he saw them no more. [22]

The "terrifying spectacle" of these spectral children, displaying
their mutilation in a theatrical tableau, is an extreme version of
the spectacle of all the children we have looked at. Visually over-
powering but inwardly opaque, they visit humanity only to be
seen. These self-presenting aliens indict adults by their remote-
ness from them. Supposedly the source of an organically integrated life, Victorian children are actually represented as impen-
etrable images that adults can look at but never absorb.

Henry James's admirers do not want to read *The Turn of the
Screw* as a ghost story—the Master is too "modern," too psycho-
logically acute, to stoop to clinking Victorian machinery—but
its account of an equivocal, unbreakable affinity between children and ghosts makes it a chilling commentary on Victorian
representations of children. Like all Victorian ghosts, Quint and
Jessel position themselves as spectacles: their props are a tower, a
window, a staircase, a desk—domestic objects they transform
into theatrical backdrops against which they strike attitudes.
Similarly, Miles and Flora are tireless pictorial players at childhood, showing but never revealing themselves, materializing before their bemused audience-governess like stage children "as ti-
gers and as Romans, . . . as Shakespeareans, astronomers and
navigators," as everything they choose to become. "We lived in a
cloud of music and affection and success and private theatricals.
The schoolroom piano broke into all gruesome fancies; and when
that failed there were confabulations in corners, with a sequel of
one of them going out in the highest spirits in order to 'come in'
as something new." [23]

The governess' obsessed spectatorship of Miles and Flora is
not, in its cultural context, pathological. Haunted by haunted

children, she is the archetypal Victorian reader-adult, watching, perhaps inventing, children real to her only as stage children, "interesting" when they imbibe the distant authority of ghosts.

GHOSTLY CHILDREN ANNOUNCE their separateness from watching humanity; the real children to whom fantasy literature appeals are equally separate beings, colonizing fantastic countries adults need but cannot reenter. Lewis Carroll's Alice in her garden; Stevenson's Jim Hawkins on his pirate ship or his deliciously ill narrator of A Child's Garden of Verses who lives in the Land of Counterpane; Christina Rossetti's Lizzie in Goblin Market, eating poisonously delicious fruit that grows in no soil adults can cultivate; Kipling's Mowgli learning the jungle's laws or his Kim playing secret games in India; George MacDonald's children enthralled by powerful fairies—all wove promises for Victorian adults, who made themselves believe in childhood countries where the self was at home and at peace.

By the end of the century these magic countries that claimed to be childhood's own owed more to the theater than they did to nature. Pantomime, melodrama, and extravaganza inspired the exotic landscapes, the incessant transformations, that made up children's charmed birthright. But adults cannot return to these countries as they do to the pantomime: actors in their essence, only children can find their way there. When they lose that way, they lose themselves. J. M. Barrie puts it most cruelly in his novelization of Peter Pan. In Neverland, the lost boys are not lost at all, but once they have grown up into exile, they are gone indeed: "You see that judge in a wig coming out at the iron door? That used to be Tootles. The bearded man who doesn't know any story to tell his children was once John."[24] The child is not the father to the man; like the very queer small boy who confronts the eminent adult Dickens, he is a lost self and another order of being.

Robert Louis Stevenson writes nostalgically in A Child's Garden of Verses of "all the thousand things that children are." Peter

Pan, a juvenile spirit of nature and an immortal creature of the theater, is those thousand things: he epitomizes the belief in a universal child that was so beloved an idea in the nineteenth century, and so disturbing a reality. Memory is the great virtue of this child-evoking literature; only memory can reclaim the lost child and heal the self. But though everyone in his story remembers Peter, Peter's own memory barely exists. The play ends even more cruelly than the novel, on a note of disturbance, not reconciliation: the year after the Darling children return home, Peter takes Wendy back to the Neverland for spring cleaning. The reluctantly growing girl hopes to restore herself, in Wordsworthian fashion, by remembering their exploits, but Peter has forgotten his own legend:

> WENDY: Fancy your forgetting the lost boys, and even Captain Hook!
> PETER: Well, then?
> WENDY: I haven't seen Tink this time.
> PETER: Who?
> WENDY: Oh dear! I suppose it is because you have so many adventures.
> PETER: (relieved): 'Course it is.

Peter's triumph of seductive coercion was his power to make jaded audiences believe in fairies, but, decomposing, he forgets even the Tinker Bell he made us clap for. In a late stage direction, Barrie associates his aphasia with his deathly nature: "In a sort of way he understands what she means . . . , but in most sorts of ways he doesn't. It has something to do with the riddle of his being. If he could get the hang of the thing his cry might become 'To live would be an awfully big adventure!' but he can never quite get the hang of it, and so no one is as gay as he."[25] Peter may seem to embody the best self of everyone forced by time and growth to leave him, but, in an ending so unsettling it is rarely staged, "the riddle of his being" makes him disappear into his own changes.

Peter's forgetfulness distinguishes him from the typical Victorian ghost who is a monument to memory, displaying itself as the unburied past, baring its wounds, intoning its admonitions, to a world that tries to forget. But in his alienation from the human world he lures, Peter Pan joins our other child-ghosts. Like so many Victorian children, he is more specter than self, assuming magical authority through an affinity with death. Only after Barrie had tried to leave *Peter Pan* behind could he fully locate the Neverland and identify his lost boys. His World War I play, *A Well-Remembered Voice*, features a dead soldier describing a death so lifelike that, in its proximity to humanity but distance from it, it blurs into childhood's country, the Neverland:

> But when one has been at the Front for a bit, you can't think how thin the veil seems to get; just one layer of it. . . . We sometimes mix up those who have gone through with those who haven't. . . . I don't remember being hit, you know. I don't remember anything till the quietness came. When you have been killed it suddenly becomes very quiet; quieter even than you have ever known it at home. Sunday used to be a pretty quiet day at my tutor's, when Trotter and I flattened out on the first shady spot up the river; but it is quieter than that.[26]

Death and ideal boyhood fade into each other; the memory of the dead, like Peter's memory, is not troubled with anything that comes between.

But is Peter the boy he crows he is? Barrie's 1904 play is, in its original conception, far more unsettling than his hazily sentimental novelization of 1911. Onstage, Peter's indeterminacy is realized by the adult woman who traditionally plays him. Wendy, who likes to categorize, calls him "boy" when she first meets him, but the audience sees an adult woman playing boyhood. Victorian England's most famous and in some ways most representative boy traditionally appears to us as, in age and gender, *not* a boy, but a vehicle of unsettling metamorphoses.

The first Peter Pan, Nina Boucicault, was striking because she was sad. Denis Mackail describes her as a compound of negations:

> The best, as no one has ever questioned, because of this haunting, eerie quality, this magic, and this sadness which is a kind of beauty too. Others will be more boyish, or more principal-boyish, or gayer and prettier, or more sinister and inhuman, or more ingeniously and painstakingly elfin. . . . But Miss Boucicault was the Peter of all Peters . . . She was unearthly but she was real. She obtruded neither sex nor sexlessness, which has so far beaten everyone else. Above all she had the touch of heart-breaking tragedy that is there in the story or fable from beginning to end; yet she never seemed to know it.[27]

This description of a mournful Peter, memorable for everything she is not, evokes not only the loss at the heart of all stories about childhood, but the loss for Victorian adults of their idea of childhood as a charmed fortification of the mercurial adult self. The adult actress is a chastening reminder that no matter how well she acts, she is no boy. If Peter Pan, in flight from mothering, might be a mother himself, that quintessence of boys never existed at all.

In nineteenth-century pantomime, which *Peter Pan* both echoes and parodies, the Principal Boy is played by a strapping woman, but pantomime, that festival of ritual transformations, has a reassuring regularity we do not find in *Peter Pan:* we know who all the pantomime characters will become, but we do not know whether Peter will metamorphose into unrecognizability or disappear altogether. Most productions of *Peter Pan* do their best to make its transformations as reassuringly predictable as those of pantomime. Captain Hook, for instance, is generally played by the same actor who plays Mr. Darling, giving us a comprehensible Freudian villain we can hate with glib relish. But in the unsettling stage directions Barrie added to the published version of the play in 1928, Hook's double is not a heavy father. When Peter saves Tiger Lily by mimicking Hook's voice, the stage direction is Barrie's own admission of personal disturbance; it tells us that Peter "can imitate the captain's voice so perfectly that even the author has a dizzy feeling that at times he was really HOOK" (act III, p. 85). More darkly still, in the tableau that follows Peter's final triumphant conquest of Hook, Barrie inserts an Orwellian image beyond the play: "The curtain rises to show PETER a very Napoleon on his ship. It must not rise again lest we see him on the poop in HOOK's hat and cigars, and with a small iron claw" (act V, scene 1, p. 132).

The implications of these arresting stage directions rarely become part of the play—the curtain "must not rise again"—but they make explicit the play's pervasive awareness of the danger of worshiping a child who is by nature a stage child (and that nature itself is theater). Infinitely mobile, never becoming the boy he will not stop playing, if the curtain were allowed to rise again, Peter could play his opposite, Hook, as easily as he plays himself. The higher reality Peter seems to bring through the window evaporates before his tendency to dissolve into the maimed adulthood from which he was supposed to free us.

But this Ur-child is, in his origin, not a child at all. In *The Little White Bird,* where he makes his first appearance, he wanders alone in a limbo, vacillating between being child or bird or fairy, but outcast from all; only after the fairies take pity on him and teach him to fly does he crystallize into the powerful being we know. This story of an Ur-child is essentially about a being so slippery it is nothing. It is also about the elusive association between children and fairies, whose natures are akin in that they are non-natures, always sliding into other orders of being. Fairies, for instance, like to disappear into flowers: "They dress exactly like flowers, and change with the seasons, putting on white when lilies are in and blue for blue-bells, and so on. . . . Most of the flowers [in the Fairy Basin] are really flowers, but some of them are fairies. You can never be sure of them, but a good plan is to walk by looking the other way, and then turn round sharply."[28] But the deceptions of fairies have their origin in the fragmentation and mutability of our own origin. Barrie's version of Genesis, published in *The Little White Bird* before it became famous in *Peter Pan*, is an origin myth even more unsettling than Darwin's: "When the first baby laughed for the first time, his laugh broke into a million pieces, and they all went skipping about. That was the beginning of fairies" (p. 160).

WE HAVE COME A LONG WAY from Jane Eyre and Pip's discoveries of apparent mighty selves. Our holy source, who keeps us whole, explodes into beings who in turn dissolve into non-being. Fearful Victorians could not rest in childhood. They gathered their energies and made the leap that promised to sanctify maturity: the leap into conversion.

# · CHAPTER II ·

## *Patterns of Conversion*

## Exhortations

I held it truth, with him who sings
   To one clear harp in divers tones,
   That men may rise on stepping-stones
Of their dead selves to higher things.[1]

The inspirational quatrain with which Tennyson's *In Memoriam* begins guided generations of Victorians. These seemingly serene lines assure us that we can grow up. Tennyson makes no mention of women, who are no doubt already heavenly, but his vowels embrace weary men, encouraging them to develop purposefully, to rise, to go higher. Even to a poet of mourning, change need not be loss. Like so much Victorian literature of development, *In Memoriam* represents growth as a series of conversions that ends in an achieved and unified self. The opening quatrain relies on an unnamed authority whose work, and presumably whose being as well, exude reassuring unity: the "divers tones" come from "*one* clear harp." Tennyson's oracle is as integral, as unperplexing, as the Shakespeare Matthew Arnold made into a mountain. Maturity, he assures us, is unity.

But like the child who only seemed to restore our lost wholeness, Tennyson's oracle is a will-o'-the-wisp. The source of his authority is oracularly unforthcoming: is he God or Goethe? Can we or can we not look up his fortifying words for ourselves? The speaker's own state of belief is equally elusive. He "held" it truth, but when? Does he still? If not, why not? Might the single-souled, clear-harped singer be one of the poet's own dead selves on whose corpse he claims he is rising? And if so, is his supposedly timeless wisdom only a phantom from the dead past? On the one hand, these lines promise developmental stability achieved by systematic progress; on the other, their wisdom evaporates in an endless process of becoming and killing what one has become. The mature and stable self dissolves into "dead selves" who point toward coherence but signify only themselves.

Tennyson's speaker cannot, it seems, affirm himself without bringing another self to life so that he may kill it. This violence and discontinuity inform all the conversions that shock Victorians into ripeness. Like the child who, in his closeness to death, seemed to guarantee the self's integrity, the adult rising to wisdom on his dead selves threatens to explode before he can save himself and his trusting reader. The child who seemed so treasured a repository of readers' eternal selfhoods vanished on examination into a fantasia of stage gestures. In the same theatrical spirit, development toward maturity resembles the ruthless self-obliterations and self-creations of the actor.

Tennyson's lines about stepping-stones and dead selves bring to wishful, equivocal life the ideal of conversion through which Victorians catapulted themselves into adulthood. Conversion, that volatile transition Jerome H. Buckley calls "the little death-in-life, the dying unto the corrupted self," is the paradigmatic Victorian passage to maturity.[2] It is generally secular in content, but religious in its faith in its own magnitude: "higher things" are not benedictions from without, but trophies of the poet's own spiritual prowess.

This mutation into being was called, optimistically, "development," whose grandeur Carlyle exalts in *Heroes and Hero Worship:*

> And yet, I say, there is an irrepressible tendency in every man to develop himself according to the magnitude which Nature has made him of; to speak-out, to act-out, what Nature has laid in him. This is proper, fit, inevitable; nay it is a duty, and even the

summary of duties for a man. The meaning of life here on earth might be defined as consisting in this: To unfold your *self,* to work what thing you have the faculty for. It is a necessity for the human being, the first law of our existence.[3]

The unfolding self and great creating Nature magnify each other. In the same sternly proud spirit, the bildungsroman, that quintessentially Victorian genre, is translated as "the novel of development." Even Darwin's controversial *On the Origin of the Species,* whose rhythm of successive mutations *In Memoriam* anticipates, was popularly said to advocate the "Development [not the 'evolutionary'] Hypothesis."

But "development" is a misleadingly integrated word for the convolutions Victorians represent as growth. Darwin's gradualism, which insisted that evolutionary change was painstakingly slow, in fact imperceptible to the scrutiny of many generations, was a similar implausible check to the catastrophic tendency of his vision. As George Levine puts it, "latent if repressed in Darwinian nature were great gaps requiring the great leaps Darwin needed to deny."[4] Among evolutionists, "development" superseded only gradually the French "transformisme" (transformation) or the "transmutation" of which Darwin wrote in an early autobiographical fragment.[5] Transformations and transmutations, in nature and in the self, can destroy and renew themselves forever, with none of the assured ascent "development" implies. Gillian Beer writes suggestively of the "enhanced recognition of complex possibilities which may be figured as conversion, transformation, or metamorphosis—or reversion" (Beer, p. 141). Whether the initiator of transformation is Darwinian nature or Carlylean man, the process that appears to be a development toward supreme integration has the potential to explode into undirected metamorphic energy.

The incessant transformations, touched with magic, underlying the official upward thrust of the Development Hypothesis echo the wonderful metamorphoses that structure Victorian pantomime and extravaganza. In the extravaganza *Once Upon a Time There Were Two Kings* (1858), for example, the inanimate swells into the living with a mere touch, by a princess, on a nosegay of magic gillyflowers: "Part of the bank changes to a Cow—a milking pail and stool rise near her,"[6] a stage direction that recalls Terry Castle's "timeless place where 'whirl is King,' a world of dizzying transformation and intoxicating variety," the theatricality of the carnival.[7] In his darkest moods, Tennyson contemplates a nature, and a human nature, composed of the same incessant transformations, but theatrical paradises are nature's and the poet's hell:

> There rolls the deep where grew the tree.
> O earth, what changes hast thou seen!
> There where the long street roars, hath been
> The stillness of the central sea.
>
> The hills are shadows, and they flow
> From form to form, and nothing stands:
> They melt like mist, the solid lands,
> Like clouds they shape themselves and go.
>
> (123, ll. 1–8)

In the face of this fluid interchange among forms, the poet insists on his steadfast spirit—"But in my spirit will I dwell, / And dream my dream, and hold it true" (123, ll. 9–10)—but the nightmare remains: the decomposing universe of modern science leaves us a nature, and a self, as infirm as theatrical display.

Although the pattern of conversion that shapes so many Victorian novels and biographies is fueled by this hope of orderly progress to spiritual immutability, it is also troubled by fear of incessant theatrical metamorphoses. Victorians cast their life cycles into inspirational allegories. In theory, maturity was the reward of a solemn ritual of conversion, whose religious content is translated into simultaneous self-destruction and self-glorification: dead selves are the price of conquering adulthood.

But the perpetually dying self, like the hills and mountains Tennyson laments, might be nothing more than shadows of its own recurrent deaths.

Even Jerome Buckley's authoritative anatomy of the "pattern of conversion," which he sees as a stabilizing crux in Victorian ideas of development, isolates the recurrent, and recurrently violent, baptisms in fire and water through which we die into ourselves (Buckley, pp. 96–108). His best-known example, Carlyle's sage Teufelsdröckh in *Sartor Resartus,* whose development became a paradigm for strong, self-making men, forges himself in a cataclysm of fire that looks suspiciously like a theatrical hell: "'Let it come, then; I will meet and defy it!' And as I so thought, there rushed like a stream of *fire* over my whole soul; and I shook base Fear away from me forever. I was strong, of unknown strength; a spirit, almost a god. Ever from that time, the temper of my misery was changed: not Fear or whining Sorrow was it, but Indignation and grim *fire*-eyed Defiance" (*Sartor,* in Carlyle, p. 127; my italics).

Like so many men before and since, Teufelsdröckh is converted to belief in himself alone, but *is* he himself or the transmuting fire? Made porous by conversion, Teufelsdröckh boasts that he is most himself when he is on the verge of dissolving into something nonhuman.

In *In Memoriam* too the moment of conversion is a moment of near dissolution. Buckley defines Victorian conversion as a self-transcendence that is, in Victorian texts, more a postulate than a dramatized reality: "The soul's abiding hope lay in its conversion from the tyranny of self to the higher purposes of the 'eternal process'" (Buckley, p. 91). Such a hope underlies the climactic section 95 of *In Memoriam,* where, in a fuzzy nocturnal vision, the poet feels he is "touch'd" by a superior soul—perhaps God's, perhaps his dead friend's, perhaps the earth's. Descending from his healing trance, he is sure of nothing beyond his own transformation, a transformation made possible by his dissolution into a force still more mysterious than the fire that remade Teufels-dröckh:

> Vague words! but ah, how hard to frame
>   In matter-moulded forms of speech,
>   Or even for intellect to reach
> Thro' memory *that which I became;*
>
> (95, ll. 45–48; my italics)

The "eternal process" evaporates; the "tyranny of self" remains, though that self is transmuted into something unimaginable. Torn as it is, the self is all we have, and it is only our own when it is in the process of becoming something else.

The climax of *In Memoriam* offers as salvation the actor's creed as well as the dying person's: we can become something greater than we were. Popular wisdom abounded in exhortations to self-transformation. From the 1820s on, reflexive locutions like "self-culture," "self-help," and "self-development" cheered Victorian men on the path to success.[8] "Self-reverence, self-knowledge, self-control" became a popular Tennysonian placebo for spiritual turbulence: in his *Oenone* these alone provide the "sovereign power" that soothes discord, war, and inflamed eroticism. Only the self is mighty enough to repair its own ravages, and it does so by mighty self-destruction.

The pattern of conversion that Victorian prophets claimed would lead to achieved adulthood might also produce a being as mutable as the shadowy, heartbreaking universe against which the integrated spirit was supposed to provide fortification. The pattern of conversion is kinetic by definition, though eighteenth-century fiction confronts more baldly the mutability inherent in conversion literature. David Marshall, for example, writes evocatively about Defoe's Moll Flanders: "Defoe recognized that the structure of autobiography and the literature of conversion would represent only one change of identity in a series of impersonations, disguises, and transformations. Passing from role to role, changing identities as if they were costumes, Moll Flanders seems to enact a [continual] cycle of death and regeneration."[9]

In Jonas Barish's comprehensive account of antitheatricalism, to change is itself to fall. Predicated on changes, the literature of conversion is by definition a literature of theatricality: "To change, clearly [for Puritan teachers] is to fall, to reenact the first change whereby Lucifer renounced his bliss and man alienated himself from the Being in whose unchanging image he was created. As a result, the actor, his trade founded on change, becomes a lively image of fallen man, the one who renews the primal degradation every day of his life, and so places himself beyond the pale."[10]

The promise of Victorian maturity, that "men may rise on stepping-stones / Of their dead selves to higher things," was at heart another warning of man's fall into theatricality. When novelists depicted bravura conversions, they accordingly tempered the spectacle sages glorified, of a self killing and renewing itself into adulthood.

CONVERSION, as Victorian prophets represent it, is fraught with unacknowledged peril because it forces us back to the stormy self it is supposed to stabilize. This religion, lacking dogma and divinity, brings a self-aggrandizement that is also self-imprisonment. Teufelsdröckh might celebrate his own development forever, but the editor of his chaotic autobiography watches his "Fermentation" apprehensively, hoping his hero's spiritual gyrations will justify themselves by some "progressive" conclusion. Long before Darwin's *Origin*, Carlyle imposes the vocabulary of evolution on the volcanic activities of the developing self:

> Under this strange nebulous envelopment, wherein our Professor has now shrouded himself, no doubt but his spiritual nature is nevertheless progressive, and growing: for how can the "Son of Time," in any case, stand still? We behold him, through those dim years, in a state of crisis, of transition: his mad Pilgrimings, and

general solution into aimless Discontinuity, what is all this but a
mad Fermentation; wherefrom, the fiercer it is, the clearer product will one day evolve itself? (*Sartor*, in Carlyle, p. 121).

The editor's fear of fermentation without resolution will
trouble the next generation of novelists. We never know whether
*Sartor*'s mystic hero does become a "clearer product"; only beyond
the boundaries of the narrative does he evolve into whatever form
he finally takes. For all we know, Teufelsdröckh continues to ferment long after we close his book; sages are licensed to ferment
indefinitely. Heroes in novels, however, must resolve their turbulence into a "clearer product" before the end of their story. To
display that product, whose clarity is the token of the novel's success, fictional protagonists generally end their development by
getting married. If the self cannot rest, it must, as far as the
reader can see, learn how to be quiet.

In fiction, marriage, not "mad Pilgrimings, and general solution into aimless Discontinuity," terminates the process of conversion. For men and women alike, the discovery of the right
mate not only neutralizes the dangerously detonating self by splitting it in two; it sets an evolutionary seal on that self's theatrical
explosiveness. Feminist critics have complained so long and so
well about the marriages that finish off the heroines of Victorian
novels that we ignore the shrouds of domestic bliss that muffle
heroes. These marriages fix the self as "the clearer product" Teufelsdröckh's editor hopes to make of him. Ideally if not actually,
they ratify the ascent implicit in the word "development," sup-
pressing the potential endlessness that turns "development" into
"transformation."

*David Copperfield*, the best-known and most influential Victorian fiction of growth to male maturity, begins by claiming to
be a Carlylean parable of self-making. In the famous opening section, David, like Teufelsdröckh, defines himself in relation to his
own possible heroism and brings himself to birth in a cosmos
fraught with omens and portents. Long before the happy end,

however, David Copperfield's history mutates into a story not of solitary heroism, but of marriage. David's destiny and identity root themselves in other characters, most of whom are women. With each of these women David is half of a tightly knit, mutually dependent dyad, so that his passage from his mother to Peggotty to little Em'ly to Aunt Betsey to Dora and finally to the absolute closure of Agnes' celestial embrace becomes a development with little transformation. David's condition is always the same; only the women on whom he fixes his identity change. He does not ferment interminably, as Teufelsdröckh does; he evolves only insofar as he puts himself into the hands of different, cherishing makers.

David's passivity has irritated many readers, but it soothes us in ways we may not consciously acknowledge, protecting us from the chaos of transformation in our understanding of a life. In this protective spirit, David assures us that his final marriage to Agnes terminates, not only his story, but himself. After praising her skill at creating him ("What I am, you have made me, Agnes"), he celebrates a marriage that ends development: "Clasped in my embrace, I held the source of every worthy aspiration I had ever had; the centre of myself, the circle of my life, my own, my wife; my love of whom was founded on a rock!"[11] He marries less a woman than his own immutable self, the self women were molding all along.

No ending could be more consummate than this one, but suddenly, David sees a ghost. Imbibing security of being through Agnes, he loses himself nevertheless. The actor who had always told his own story dwindles into his own audience: "We stood together in the same old-fashioned window at night, when the moon was shining; Agnes with her quiet eyes raised up to it; I following her glance. Long miles of road then opened out before my mind; and, toiling on, I saw a ragged way-worn boy, forsaken and neglected, who should come to call even the heart now beating against mine, his own" (p. 937). Like the Dickens of the autobiographical fragment, the supposedly mature David is haunted by an apparition who is his young self, undermining in his detachment the man's apparent achieved stability. The child of whom it was predicted "that I was privileged to see ghosts and spirits" (p. 49) becomes the ghost of everything exemplary development discards.

David marries Agnes; the rest of the plot falls into place, but the consummated hero loses his "I." Instead of rejoicing in his intact being, he becomes an observer of the spectacle of his life: "I see myself, with Agnes at my side, journeying along the road of life. I see our children and our friends around us; and I hear the roar of many voices, not indifferent to me as I travel on" (p. 946). The marriage that was supposed to shield the self precipitates the fading of that self into its own audience.

*David Copperfield* is the quintessential representation of the marriage with which Victorian fiction tries to shore up the developing self against its own metamorphic potential. It is also, in the theatrical doubling and involutions that invade its syntax at the end, the quintessential repudiation of that marriage. David's spectatorship of his own rituals of bliss anticipates a literature in which marriage cannot put a fermenting identity to rest. The disruptions the Victorian novel indicates but cannot accommodate find their dark expression in Gothic fiction, which is often predicated on an unholy amalgam of marriage and metamorphosis. Bram Stoker's Dracula, is of course an agent of transformations he calls marriages, but Oliver Onions, a subtler if more obscure horror writer than Stoker, goes beyond monstrosities to depict as universal a turmoil no marriage can settle.

We never know whether Onions' possessed protagonists are haunted by actual specters or by their own personified desires. Bessie in "The Lost Thyrsus" is a young woman wavering between marriage to a stable clod and erotic visions of ancient Bacchanalian transformations. Her fiancé thinks her mad; she thinks Greek spirits are haunting her; but the narrator assures us that the true agent of transformation is an uncontainable self common to us all, a self that makes marriage an impossible resolution. "Again the high dinning calls of 'Hasten! Hasten!' were mingled with the deeper 'Beware!' She knew in her soul that, once over that terrible edge, the Dream would become the Reality and the Reality the Dream. She knew nothing of the fluidity of the thing called Personality—not a thing at all, but a state, a balance, a relation, a resultant of forces so delicately in equilibrium that a touch, and—*pff!*—the horror of Formlessness rushed over all."[12] In Oliver Onions' oracular dismissal of an integral self, neither marriage nor love can contain "the fluidity" of "Personality," within which lies "the horror of Formlessness" that novels like *David Copperfield* dispel and evoke. This fluidity is the horror at the heart of all Victorian prophecy, though only Gothicism confronts it fully.

Oliver Onions and other Gothic writers subvert high Victorian hopes that maturity in the form of marriage will produce an integrated and stable self. The theater was licensed to laugh at the assumptions underlying the ending of *David Copperfield*, which does its best to convince us that its hero is consummately created by the right marriage. W. S. Gilbert's corrosive farce *Engaged* (1877) asks a darkly related question about character: if marriage makes the self, does un-marriage un-make it?

Until the final curtain of *Engaged*, none of the six central characters knows whether he or she is married or, if so, to whom. Its great moment is Belinda Treherne's eloquent affirmation that she is no one:

> Say, rather, horror—distraction—chaos! Perhaps he was already married; in that case, I am a bigamist. Maybe he is dead; in that case, I am a widow. Maybe he is alive; in that case, I am a wife. *What am I?* Am I single? Am I married? Am I a widow? Can I marry? Have I married? May I marry? *Who am I? Where am I? What am I?—What is my name?* What is my condition in life? If I am married, to whom am I married? If I am a widow, how came I

to be a widow, and whose widow came I to be? Why am I his widow? What did he die of? Did he leave me anything?[13]

This torrent of possible identities convinces us that no marriage can tell Belinda's inchoate selves who or what she is. She is all things and no things; the other side of the self made is the self unmade. *Engaged* carries to its logically absurd conclusion sensation dramas like *East Lynne* and *Aurora Floyd,* in which the marriages that determine the identities of all the characters are flimsy legal fictions, undone with ludicrous ease by the return of a prior mate. In all these plays the contingency of marriage produces chaos in the self. In the shadow worlds of Gothic fiction and the theater the fixity David Copperfield appears to achieve is shown to rest on a fluidity so frightening and so funny no ending can contain it. Gilbert's Belinda embodies the infinite malleability of all the potential beings Victorian novels do their best, in their endings, to complete.

David Copperfield and other male protagonists act out what was supposed to be the destiny of actual Victorian women: his conversion brings him a fixed self through perfect marriage. Women writers, though, rely less than men on a marriage that generates the best self. Exhorted on all sides to complete themselves by marrying, allowed no official identities other than those of daughter, wife, and mother, Victorian women rarely affirm this ideology in their novels, nor did actual women adhere to it in their conversions to adulthood. Florence Nightingale recognized her epic destiny only after time had freed her from rescuing men. On New Year's Eve 1852 she wrote in her journal: "all my admirers are married . . . and I stand with all the world before me . . . It has been a baptism of fire this year."[14] Conversions by women rarely involve worship of another. In novels they often occur in an interlude apart from the propulsion of the marriage plot, in which the heroine is converted away from love and authority to the integrity of her own consciousness.

At the end of Elizabeth Gaskell's *North and South,* for example, the powerful heroine Margaret Hale finds herself utterly, if temporarily, bereft of authorities. Her ineffectual parents have died; the mutinous brother she adores is forced into exile; she has rejected two masterful suitors; death has just taken her final guardian, a doting godfather, leaving her under the demeaning protection of shallow London relations. The marriage plot hovers to rescue her from independence, but first she experiences a moment of conversion more powerful, if less rhetorically ornate, than Teufelsdröckh's fire-baptism, less self-abandoned if more momentary than David Copperfield's:

> When they returned to town, Margaret fulfilled one of her sea-side resolves, and took her life into her own hands. Before they went to Cromer, she had been as docile to her aunt's laws as if she were still the scared little stranger who cried herself to sleep that first night in the Harley Street nursery. But she had learnt, in those solemn hours of thought, that she must one day answer for her own life, and what she had done with it; and she tried to settle that most difficult problem for women, how much was to be utterly merged in obedience to authority, and how much might be set apart for freedom in working. . . . So Margaret gained the acknowledgment of her right to follow her own ideas of duty. [15]

In "those solemn hours of thought," if not in sustained action, Margaret learns the lessons of Victorian sages, which Gaskell puts more uncompromisingly than the sages do: conversion is self-conversion, and the self may be all-sufficing. In this interlude beyond her plot Margaret Hale achieves the self-worship implicit in the conversions of male heroes.

The affinity between the conversions of men and women lies in this potential limitlessness. All are profoundly private; at the same time, all are deeply theatrical. Tennyson's speaker's entranced exaltation, Teufelsdröckh's "unknown strength" that inflates him into "a spirit, almost a god," David Copperfield's marriage prayer to his perfected self, Margaret Hale's solemnly disobedient self-possession, all involve not so much conversions to new beliefs as self-transformations into awesome objects of belief. This power of the self to swell into sacredness is the essence of the Victorian actor's art. The *process* of transforming oneself into "almost a god," as Carlyle calls it, honors a theatricality at the heart of the Victorian pattern of conversion. In solemn privacy and on the stage, the self mutates into the answer to its own prayer.

The theatricality of *North and South,* and of similar novels by women, is subtly different from the theatricality a male tradition fears. Carlyle and Tennyson do their best to solidify a self besieged by eruptions and mutations; Dickens assures the integrity of his David by marrying him to "a rock." Margaret Hale, however, is threatened less by the inundation of multiple selves than by the potential public power of her transfiguration. A crowded moment of self-realization produces, in its compound of theatricality, political rage, violent eroticism, ambition, and guilt, the most extraordinary love scene in British Victorian fiction.

Margaret has begun to fall in love with the Manchester mill owner Mr. Thornton, though his economic ruthlessness appalls her. A strike is in progress; a desperate mob gathers around Mr. Thornton's mill. Identifying with the fury of the oppressed, Margaret taunts Thornton into confronting his workers: "If you have any courage or noble quality in you, go out and speak to them, man to man!" (p. 232).

Goaded, he does so; the hands surround him murderously; Margaret flings herself into the crowd, shielding him with her body. A worker throws a stone, cutting her forehead. Before she faints, her wound disperses the mob: "They were watching, openeyed, and open-mouthed, the thread of dark-red blood which wakened them up from their trance of passion" (p. 235). Her rush into the public, violent streets makes Margaret, for one intense scene, not only a ruler of men but a charismatic spectacle among them.

Seeing her dead, as he thinks, Thornton plunges into the love that begins his conversion. Their momentary physical intimacy haunts him: "Everything seemed dim and vague beyond—behind—besides the touch of her arms round his neck—the soft clinging which made the dark colour come and go in his cheek as he thought of it" (p. 244). Margaret, equally moved, is haunted not by intimate touches, but by memories of her metamorphosis into a public woman: "She could not be alone, prostrate, powerless as she was,—a cloud of faces looked up at her, giving her no idea of fierce vivid anger, or of personal danger, but a deep sense of shame that she should thus be the object of universal regard— a sense of shame so acute that it seemed as if she would fain have burrowed into the earth to hide herself, and yet she could not escape out of that unwinking glare of many eyes" (pp. 248–249).

Like David Copperfield, Thornton is converted into love when he collapses into intimacy, losing his grip on his public role; Margaret is catapulted out of seclusion, into the "unwinking glare of many eyes." For a Victorian woman, officially consigned to private life, this stellar appearance on the streets carries a glory, vertigo, and shame that are less akin to Teufelsdröckh's rejoicing in his soul's perfection than they are to the Victorian actress Ellen Terry feeling, for the first time, like a star:

> I had had some success in other parts, and had tasted the delight of knowing the audiences liked me, and had liked them back again. But never until I appeared as Portia at the Prince of Wales's had I experienced that awe-struck feeling which comes, I suppose, to no actress more than once in a life-time—the feeling of the conqueror. In homely parlance, I knew that I had "got them" at the moment when I spoke the speech beginning, "You see me, Lord Bassanio, where I stand."
>
> "What can this be?" I thought. "*Quite* this thing has never come to me before! *This is different!* It has never been quite the same before."
>
> It was never to be quite the same again.
>
> Elation, triumph, being lifted on high by a single stroke of the mighty wing of glory—call it by any name, think of it as you

like—it was as Portia that I had my first and last sense of it. And, while it made me happy, it made me miserable because I foresaw, as plainly as my own success, another's failure [that of her Shylock, Charles Coghlan].[16]

For a woman, metamorphosis into public life can be depicted only in the language of conquest, though like Ellen Terry, Margaret Hale knows that her public power is ephemeral: men may be conquerors and heroes all the time, but women can burst into power only for charmed moments. Ellen Terry achieves her moment only when, as Portia, she relinquishes herself to her triumphant wooer Bassanio; moreover, the actress cannot forget that her "mighty wing of glory" sweeps a male colleague to failure.[17] Like Ellen Terry's, Margaret Hale's elation at conquest modulates into shame, in part because it rests on the concurrent humiliation of a man.[18]

But since Margaret Hale is not an actress, Gaskell makes her bleed for her conquest. Margaret's wound, not Margaret herself, smites the mob with awe and Mr. Thornton with love: the workers retreat at her blood, while their employer collapses into passion at the pallor of her apparent death. At the pinnacle of her shame and glory, Margaret takes on the attributes of a fearfully loved Victorian female type who is both charismatic invalid and female demon. In this intense moment her wound splits off from her consciousness, becoming the vivid emblem of her public self. The strange, almost holy power of Margaret's wound is demonically reiterated in Gaskell's eerie, seemingly uncharacteristic Gothic tale, "The Poor Clare."

Published three years after *North and South*, "The Poor Clare" is a supernatural parable of the demonic doubling Margaret Hale momentarily experiences. In "The Poor Clare," Bridget, a poor peasant, inadvertently curses her own granddaughter Lucy, who consequently acquires an evil double. This demon laughs, mocks, and parades herself, stealing all attention from the "real" Lucy, who is sedate and genteel: "Just at that instant, standing as I was opposite to her in the full and perfect morning light, I saw behind her another figure—a ghastly resemblance, complete in likeness, so far as form and feature and minutest touch of dress could go, but with a loathsome demon soul looking out of the grey eyes, that were in turns mocking and voluptuous. My heart stood still within me; every hair rose up erect; my flesh crept with horror. *I could not see the grave and tender Lucy—my eyes were fascinated by the creature beyond.*"[19]

In this "creature beyond," Gaskell personifies the fearful public self *North and South* places in a socially realistic setting, for the essence of her female demon is her scene-stealing theatricality. At one point she mimics Bridget's tragic gestures extravagantly, thereby forcing Bridget to an awareness of her own performance of suffering; her power is the ambiguous gift of comic transformation. This vibrantly performing double makes "The Poor Clare" one of the few anticipations of *Dracula* written by a woman; it is also, with its laughing, mocking devil, a compelling female anticipation of *Dr. Jekyll and Mr. Hyde*. As in *Dracula*, whose vampirized women display themselves in blood to perform charismatic rituals, the performing woman within the good woman is a spellbinding monster. Her primacy gives a darker twist to Tennyson's exhortation: men may rise to higher things on stepping-stones of their dead selves, but the dead selves of women, more alive than the living are allowed to be, will not remain mere stepping-stones. Wounded or laughing, they devour the novels that try to contain them

*North and South* is not a Gothic novel, and so Margaret Hale does not become a demon or a vampire; she marries Mr. Thornton, and, though she has become wealthy enough to repair his many mistakes, she ends in exaggerated humility. The lovers pledge themselves with characteristic Victorian competitiveness in reverence:

"Oh, Mr. Thornton [she murmurs "in a broken voice"], "I am not good enough!"

"Not good enough! Don't mock my own deep feeling of unworthiness."                                                                        (p. 527)

Marriage mutes woman and man alike. At the end Margaret and Thornton revel in unworthiness, not self-realization.

Few Victorians believe in the fixed self they claim to desire. Their hymns of renewal are galvanized by images of violent death. Tennyson's "dead selves" are more vivid than his "higher things"; the drowned Steerforth is more resonant than the married David; in *Jane Eyre*, Bertha Mason's and Rochester's shattered bodies and the ruined ancestral manor that crushed them overshadow the consecrated but dramatically unrealized union catastrophe brings about. The waste products of secular salvation are more powerful than its fruits. Like Darwin's natural selection, the pattern of conversion manifests itself in the fossils it discards.

## Lives

Elizabeth Gaskell's *The Life of Charlotte Brontë* and John Forster's *The Life of Charles Dickens* are literary biographies that acknowledge, if uneasily, the unsettled adulthoods that novels try in their various ways to resolve. The middle years of Gaskell's Charlotte Brontë and Forster's Dickens do not, in either novelist, produce an own self. Gaskell's Brontë makes and remakes herself through incessant suffering, while Forster's Dickens performs himself into near-obliteration. Both exemplify the approved activities of their gender (women suffer, men strive), but each also acts a life imaginative literature lacks the form to confront: that of a theatrical self, unable to rest in its own identity. Neither life solidifies after the conversion to art that makes both worthy of heroic biographies.

Forster's Dickens bursts into maturity with an explosion of novels, travels, periodicals, private theatricals, and domestic bustle. Gaskell's Charlotte Brontë, on the other hand, concentrates so assiduously on suffering and enduring that we can scarcely imagine her writing. Even the composition of *Jane Eyre* seems incidental to her perpetual wrenching separations from the Parsonage into servitude, and then from her siblings as they die in turn. Her life, as Gaskell presents it, is a series of catastrophes; her vocation is to endure them.

Though Charlotte Brontë was an actual public woman, unlike the heroines Gaskell imagined, she has no demonic double to bleed or laugh for her. Her wound, like her life, is inward. Describing Brontë's second trip to Brussels, Gaskell decorously omits whatever she knew about Brontë's passion for her teacher and employer, M. Heger, concentrating instead on the magnitude of her subject's "great internal struggle":

> She now felt that she had made great progress towards obtaining proficiency in the French language, which had been her main object in coming to Brussels. But to the zealous learner "Alps on Alps arise." No sooner is one difficulty surmounted than some other desirable attainment appears, and must be laboured after. A knowledge of German now became her object: and she resolved to compel herself to remain in Brussels till that was gained. The strong yearning to go home came upon her; the stronger self-denying will forbade. There was a great internal struggle; every fibre of her heart quivered in the strain to master her will; and, when she conquered herself, she remained, not like a victor calm and supreme on the throne, but like a panting, torn, and suffering victim. Her nerves and her spirits gave way. Her health became much shaken.[20]

Charlotte Brontë both exemplifies and denies Tennyson's exhortation to rise on stepping-stones of dead selves to higher things. Gaskell's image of heroic ascent—"Alps on Alps arise"—invokes perpetuity, not conquest. The tensions in her prose between the past tense and present participles suggest that the state of division and the process of suffering are unending and unend-

able: "when she conquer*ed* herself, she remain*ed*, not like a victor calm and supreme on the throne, but like a pant*ing*, torn, and
suffer*ing* victim." Charlotte Brontë's creative struggles rarely inspire such intense language, though had Gaskell chosen to con-
centrate on the actual completion of her four novels, the biography would have acquired a rhythm of conquest and closure.
Gaskell, though, prefers to turn her subject into an anguished
Everywoman whose authorship is almost incidental; her enforced
vocation is suffering, her conversions are objectless, unresolved,
and unterminated. This exemplary woman performs unendingly
a torment that will never define the self or fix it.

John Forster's Charles Dickens seems to be everything a man
should be and everything Charlotte Brontë is not. Once his subject reaches maturity, Forster gives him little inner life; there is
no "great internal struggle." Instead, the biographer exhausts
himself cataloguing Dickens' round of frenetic activities, scarcely
bothering to construct a bridge between the introspective, se-
cretly suffering child and the indefatigable adult. Dickens' own
determination seems magically to make him a man:

> Nor would it be possible to have better illustrative comment on all
> these years than is furnished by his father's reply to a friend it was
> now hoped to interest on his behalf, which more than once I have
> heard him whimsically but good-humouredly imitate. "Pray, Mr.
> Dickens, where was your son educated?" "Why, indeed, Sir—ha!
> ha!—he may be said to have educated himself!" Of the two kinds
> of education which Gibbon says that all men who rise above the
> common level receive: the first that of his teachers, and the sec-
> ond, more personal and more important, *his own*; he had the ad-
> vantage only of the last. It nevertheless sufficed for him.[21]

So much for growing up. Forster's irony toward Dickens' wayward father apes that father's genial insouciance: turning himself
into a great man is simply another of The Inimitable's tricks.
Forster's deft showman seems as far removed as possible from Gaskell's Charlotte Brontë, who wrenches herself from one phase of

agony to another, but the rhythm of his maturity is the same as hers. Like Brontë, Dickens cannot rest in what he is. His books are completed, but their author never is. As Forster's biography goes on, it reenacts Forster's own growing alienation during Dickens' lifetime, when the novelist had refused to settle into being the heroic man of letters the conventional Forster wanted to revere. Forster quotes a ruffled letter from the restless Dickens: "You are not so tolerant as perhaps you might be of the wayward and unsettled feeling which is part (I suppose) of the tenure on which one holds an imaginative life, and which I have, as you ought to know well, often only kept down by riding over it like a dragoon—but let that go by" (II, 199).

In the course of the biography (as in the course of their friendship), Forster associates the "wayward and unsettled feeling" he deplored with Dickens' deplorable theatricality. In his eyes, the lust to perform cheapened the literary man; the public readings that consumed Dickens in his last years drained his art and shortened his life. As Forster structures his biography, the diabolical theater brings about his subject's fall. Literature and performing are fastidiously segregated into "higher" and "lower" activities: "He took to a higher calling [as novelist], but it included the lower [as actor]. . . . He had the power of projecting himself into shapes and suggestions of his fancy which is one of the marvels of creative imagination, and what he desired to express he became. The assumptions of the theatre have the same method at a lower pitch, depending greatly on personal accident; but the accident as much as the genius favored Dickens, and another man's conception underwent in his acting the process which in writing he applied to his own" (I, 374).

In Forster's morality play Dickens the actor, who became the "shapes and suggestions of his fancy," devoured Dickens the literary man, whose "higher calling" should have enabled him to rise above this mobility and control it. Forster's hero falls victim to theatricality: unlike his David, he does not marry "a rock" and embrace a sole and permanent identity. His restlessness drives him to be more things than a life of Dickens can contain. He alienates even his authorized biographer by refusing to rest in an assured self.

Gaskell and Forster do not freeze their subjects' lives as novelists do; both are true to theatrical selves that evade the boundaries of an assured identity. The Victorian biographer is not bound by the novelist's need to finish a life, but even the biographer of a heroic subject must confront the possibility that the idea of a life is itself a lie: the revered name and the familiar face may cloak, not a knowable identity, but undirected changes.

## Perversities: actors, monsters, lunatics, and saints

Conversion contains the seeds of perversion. That noble Victorian enterprise of mighty self-making always threatens to produce, not superior mutations, but monsters. The potential chaos of conversion underlies the obsession, in popular literature, with such hybrids as fairies, wolfmen, white rabbits with pocket watches, vampires, owls singing to responsive pussycats, all manner of unclassifiable anomalies, lost somewhere between the animal and human species. Tennyson's exhortation to self-improvement in *In Memoriam*—"Move upward, working out the beast" (118, 27)—modulates, in the 1880s and 1890s, into something like the cult of the beast. Those classics of metamorphic reversion—Stevenson's *The Strange Case of Dr. Jekyll and Mr. Hyde* (1886), H. G. Wells's *The Island of Dr. Moreau* (1896), and that great Gothic account of bestial and dead selves restored to life, Bram Stoker's *Dracula* (1897)—all feature men who are inseparable from the animals they are supposed to have risen above. In evolutionary theory, as we have seen, the progressive-sounding "development" dignifies a "transmutation" liable to produce a chaos of species. Similarly, the pattern of conversion may generate, not Tennyson's "nobler type," but a jumble of creatures whose mad metamorphoses subvert not only the primacy of humanity, but its existence.

The cult of the beast stimulated the cult of the actor. Antitheatricalism gave way to awe at a being who could be tragic and comic, high and low, saint and devil, in turn. In his years as actor-manager of the Lyceum (1878–1902), Henry Irving became the first nineteenth-century actor to court respectability *as* an actor and to win it, for he embodied in his own lean person the fascination of transformations.

Irving's Lyceum came to symbolize the opulence of the British Empire—so compellingly that when, in 1895, Irving became the first British actor to be knighted, he seemed to his acolytes to be conferring an honor upon the Queen—but most of his repertoire, including *The Bells* that rang him to stardom, consisted of pirated French plays. It seems appropriate that this imperial actor who plundered France for his material claimed as his hero, not Prince Albert or Disraeli, but Napoleon. England's last nineteenth-century hero, its devil-saint, belonged to no country.

Irving made himself appear heroically uncultivated by intensifying eccentricities of the sort more conventional actors labored to get rid of. He had no native language: he spoke like a foreigner, though one from no identifiable country. Frances Donaldson, among many others, describes "his strange manner of pronouncing the English language, and . . . an almost grotesque method of moving about the stage. Sir Henry, we are told, said 'Gud' for 'God,' 'Cut-thrut dug,' 'Tak the rup frum mey nek,' 'ritz' for 'rich,' 'seyt' for 'sight,' 'stod' for 'stood,' 'hond' or 'hend' for 'hand,' while for 'To trammel up the consequence,' he said 'tram-mele up-p the cunse-quence.' And, while so hideously distorting the language, he moved about the stage with depressed head, and protruding shoulders, making with his legs sidelong and backward skirmishes."[22]

Irving must have resembled a hybrid creature himself. Like one of the half-transformed, semiarticulate beast-men in H. G.

Wells's *The Island of Dr. Moreau,* he sidled about emitting primitive words of his own devising. One possibly apocryphal account of his Mathias in *The Bells* has him howling like a wolf. A man who was mesmerized by Irving's performance recalls: "I remember every word: 'How the wolves howl at Daniel's farm—like me they are hungry, searching for prey.' And then he howled. It makes my hair stand on end when I think of it."[23]

In his roles Irving alternated with chameleonlike ease between evil and good. As a young man he is said to have taken revenge "for the children of the whole village on an old woman who had persecuted them with threats of hell-fire by appearing at her bedside, wearing a mask, horns and a tail. However, shortly after his tenth birthday, he somewhat allayed [the] anxiety [of his ferociously Methodist mother] by falling into an ecstasy during a service and professing conversion to the religion of his fathers" (Donaldson, p. 56). As an actor he showed the same aptitude at converting himself from the diabolical to the divine. Like Teufelsdröckh, Irving rose triumphantly from spiritual depths to heights. He became famous for his guilt-stricken villains—Eugene Aram, Mathias in *The Bells*—but the rituals of sin that mesmerized audiences made him a model of respectability. At the end he sanctified himself. In the course of his overweening career he played not only Mephistopheles and Napoleon, but a mystic Dante, reconceiving the cosmos. Most venerably, he became Tennyson's exalted English saint, Thomas à Becket.

Irving's amanuensis and disciple, Bram Stoker, who managed the Lyceum from the beginning of his empire to its end, celebrated his master less as artist than magician, lord of holy transformations—just the sorts of transformations novels celebrate and snuff out. Stoker's long, worshipful biography dwells on Irving's capacity to incarnate England's pantheon of saints. Reading Tennyson's *Becket* at Canterbury Cathedral, Irving *becomes* Saint Thomas, restored from the dead to resanctify his own cathedral.

As Dante, "he did not merely look like Dante—he *was* Dante; it was like a veritable re-incarnation."[24]

As Stoker presents it, Irving's career fulfills, through Tennyson's own saint, the Tennysonian exhortation with which we began: he rises on stepping-stones of his dead selves to higher things. But like his age, Stoker is appalled as well as awed by those dead selves off whom we live. Henry Irving inspired not only Stoker's reverence, but his Dracula, a versatile vampire who is able to *become* his victims as well as eat them. Irving consecrates us all when he translates himself into Saint Thomas or Dante, but the suave Court Dracula is more memorable when he suddenly becomes a beast:

> What I saw was the Count's head coming out from the window. I did not see the face, but I knew the man by the neck and the movement of his back and arms. In any case I could not mistake the hands which I had had so many opportunities of studying. . . . But my very feelings changed to repulsion and terror when I saw the whole man slowly emerge from the window and begin to crawl down the castle wall over that dreadful abyss, *face down* with his cloak spreading out around him like great wings. At first I could not believe my eyes. I thought it was some trick of the moonlight, some weird effect of shadow; but I kept looking, and it could be no delusion. I saw the fingers and toes grasp the corners of the stones, worn clear of the mortar by the stress of years, and by thus using every projection and inequality move downwards with considerable speed, just as a lizard moves down a wall.
>
> What manner of man is this, or what manner of creature is it in the semblance of man? . . . I am encompassed about with terrors that I dare not think of. . . . [25]

"What manner of man is this, or what manner of creature is it in the semblance of man?" The actor as well as the monster elicits these urgent questions. Their range of identities is the drama, tragic or comic, of their age; Irving's sainted metamorphoses are mocked by Dracula's diabolical ones. Together, the actor and the vampire embody the horror of all the creatures man's unbounded appetite for conversion inspires him to become.

As THE THEATER grew more respectable, it rarely required its actresses to mutate from serpents to saints. On the fin-de-siècle stage women's roles tended to highlight a single attitude—nobility, innocence, or diabolism—rather than displaying the startling versatility of an Irving. The lizard slithering in suave Count Dracula, the Mr. Hyde laughing in staid Dr. Jekyll, were, like the devils lurking in Irving's saints, theatrical as well as literary sensations. But women were rarely encouraged in overtly metamorphic play. In an age of militant, disruptive feminism, in which supposedly "new" women stopped playing their assigned roles, the idea of female metamorphosis was too horrible to constitute entertainment.[26] Theater historian Cary M. Mazer finds even in the supposedly enlightened theatrical community "a genuine fear of a woman actually *acting* . . . ; of the actress finding in her own soul the freedom of emotional expression of the character she plays; of the actress being corrupted by the moral impurity of the character, or, most significantly, being corrupted by the very transgressive act of becoming someone else, of finding within herself other selves to become."[27]

In literature women's conversions were nullified by marriage or death. In life as in the theater, their capacity to become multiple selves was aligned less with metaphysical profundities than with disease. Margaret Hale's crowd-captivating wound in *North and South* is a token of the charismatic power of illness, mental or physical, in women.[28]

Diseased women could be safely cherished, even "interesting," because illness appears to be a condition of exemplary privacy, as well as an involuntary accord with the nature that is woman's sphere. Sick women are, in theory, confined; they will not sidle out of the windows of castles, inciting observers to doubt their own identities; they will not revive their dead selves onstage. But a compulsively theatrical age made a pageant even of the sick-room. In extreme instances that illuminate the norm, women's crises and conversions acquired the dynamism of theater. These crises and conversions were played out most eloquently in France.

France inspired Henry Irving's repertoire and ambiguous personae; it was also the site of histrionic activity that dramatized the range of female metamorphoses. Jean Martin Charcot's clinic at the Salpêtrière, which flourished in the decades (1870–1900) when Irving ruled the British stage, made stars of its mental patients. Madness gave them the range of identities ordinary women, onstage as well as off, were forbidden to display.

Charcot did more than watch his female hysterics: at his popular public lectures he hypnotized them into striking a series of expressive "attitudes," from religious to erotic "passion," from ecstasy to despair.[29] Pressing "hysterogenic spots" on his pliable patients, Charcot guided them into a succession of sinuous postures that hypnotized in turn the glamorous audiences at his lectures. For those who could not attend, photographs were available, just as they were for theatrical productions. As in a theatrical company, Charcot's hysterics vied with each other for primacy; one, Blanche Wittman, won the title of "Queen of Hysterics," but many others writhed and gyrated for the audience with strenuous picturesqueness. Charcot transformed that sanctum of privacy, the mad mind, into an arena of theatrical display.

George Frederick Drinka's vivid descriptions of these hysterical attitudes rely on the language and syntax of metamorphosis. He describes women performing madness by swinging among a series of selves: "*Back and forth, back and forth* [Geneviève] would go, saint to prostitute, saint to prostitute, in ten minutes. . . . *back and forth*, in and out, ecstasy, arc-en-cercle, ecstasy, erotic posturing, laughing, crying, giggling, crying, she spoke into the ears of Regnard, Bourneville, Charcot, and M. X" (Drinka, p. 94; my italics). "[Madeleine's] ecstasies transported her back to great moments in Christian history and transmuted her into great personages. In various trances she was present at the crucifixion and at the Nativity. She took on the role of Christ in the womb of Mary, and then she was the Virgin Mary herself, pregnant with God. Then she was Jesus born in the manger, Mary holding the child. *Back and forth*—God, woman, lover, sufferer—the ecstasies flowed from moment to moment" (Drinka, p. 353; my italics).

The versatility of these supposed madwomen, their mesmerizing movement back and forth between demonism and saintliness, is that of the Victorian actor as Henry Irving personified him. Their hysteria is their aptitude at conversion, from one attitude to another, from one spiritual state to another. Some, like Geneviève, claimed sisterhood with such nonhospitalized ecstatics as Louise Lateau, whose bizarre ability to bleed and heal in turn was called miraculous by churchmen, but hysterical by doctors. Louise Lateau's charismatic wounds made her a saint in the eyes of some believers, while another sick girl, the consumptive "little flower," Thérèse of Lisieux (1873–1897), was well on her way to canonization almost immediately after her protracted death; the ecstasies of her long illness brought her spiritual fame. Bernadette of Lourdes (1844–1879), the most stellar saint of the nineteenth century, combined the spectacular versatility of Charcot's patients—adoring crowds were transfixed by her wild alterations between ecstatic trances and bestial grovelings—with the charismatic consumptiveness of Thérèse. The versatility actresses were forbidden to play became, in sick women, a mesmerizing miracle.

All these women, hysterics and saints alike, became stars of disease by unfurling their multiple selves. All underwent orgiastic, dramatic, and public "conversions" that displayed their spiritual virtuosity; all transformed private moments of vision into public spectacles. Their "stardom," as madwomen or saints, was analogous to the mocking double inflicted on the sedate heroine of Elizabeth Gaskell's "The Poor Clare"; it too was a doppelgänger of the private woman, turning modesty, psychic or spiritual, into a capering spectacle. The visionary guide whom Bernadette called "the Lady of the Immaculate Conception" was a celestial mutation of Gaskell's mocking, consecrating double: the beautiful lady who appeared in a vision to the obscure Bernadette guided the young girl (and her town of Lourdes) to spectacular life, to a healing spring, and to spiritual fame.

Whether Bernadette, or Charcot's Geneviève and Madeleine, were saintly or sick, all lived the wistful creed that begins *In Memoriam:* their perpetual mutations allowed them to rise on stepping-stones of their dead selves to higher things. Since all saw themselves as saints, higher things were their constant companions. Women might be barred from heroics, relegated to the privacy of illness and solitary visions, but nineteenth-century theatricality energized those illnesses and visions with transforming glory.

THE PATTERN OF CONVERSION, so crucial an article of Victorian faith, was an extraordinarily robust belief. It brought assurance on the one hand, terror on the other. A Count crawling lizardlike down his own noble battlements; a girl whose sudden bleeding inspires her with mystic power; the still more comprehensive nightmare of a self whose mutations never end in achieved identity—all were eruptions of a horror within the forms of conventional solace.

The Victorian self refuses to stop becoming; its development produces only spectacular transformations. Its theatrical, incessant, and perhaps uncontainable energies draw it toward the death that might give it rest.

# · CHAPTER III ·

## *Death Scenes*

"To die will be an awfully big adventure," crows that eminent Edwardian Peter Pan.[1] Peter, the child who is no child, the boy-woman who is neither dead nor alive, speaks for a century of haunted adults. Victorian writers dwell on death, depicting its transformations with hungry precision, as if to rehearse for themselves and their readers that final moment—grasped at in life but withheld—when the self reveals itself wonderfully and wholly.

The deathbed scenes that were popular literary set pieces are crescendos of revelation, not of conventional afterlives, but of their dying subjects. These death scenes exemplify what Philippe Ariès calls the modern cult of death, an activity that consummates

> the discovery of the individual, the discovery, at the hour or thought of death, of one's own identity, one's personal biography, in this world as in the next. The desire to be oneself forced tombstones to emerge from their anonymity and to become commemorative monuments.
>
> At the same time this desire made the soul the essential element of the personality. Liberated from the weight of the species, the soul became the crystallization of being, the individuality itself, an individuality whose characteristics, whether good or bad, nothing could now alter.[2]

Here are some crowning Victorian deaths, chosen almost at random. In all of them, the soul—the "crystallization of being" Ariès defines—springs into life at last:

It was not till late in the afternoon, when the light was falling, that he took a hand of each in his and said, looking at Deronda, "Death is coming to me as the divine kiss which is both parting and reunion—which takes me from your bodily eyes and gives me full presence in your soul. Where thou goest, Daniel, I shall go. Is it not begun? Have I not breathed my soul into you? We shall live together."[3]

Quietly, quietly, all the lines of the plan of the great Castle melted one after another. Quietly, quietly, the ruled and cross-ruled countenance on which they were traced, became fair and blank. Quietly, quietly, the reflected marks of the prison bars and of the zig-zag iron on the wall-top, faded away. Quietly, quietly, the face subsided into a far younger likeness of her own than she had ever seen under the grey hair, and sank to rest.[4]

I could not think him dead, but his face and throat were washed with rain; the bedclothes dripped, and he was perfectly still. The lattice, flapping to and fro, had grazed one hand that rested on the sill; no blood trickled from the broken skin, and when I put my fingers to it, I could doubt no more—he was dead and stark!

I hasped the window; I combed his black long hair from his forehead; I tried to close his eyes—to extinguish, if possible, that frightful, life-like gaze of exultation, before any one else beheld it. They would not shut; they seemed to sneer at my attempts, and his parted lips and sharp, white teeth sneered too![5]

These three dying men are as different as they could be in temperament, ambition, and religion. Mordecai is a saint, William Dorrit a fraud, and Heathcliff a fiend. Mordecai believes in his vision of Zion realized as a sacred secular community; William Dorrit believes in his own illusory gentility; Heathcliff believes in ghosts. Their authors, George Eliot, Charles Dickens, and Emily Brontë, are even more disparate than their dying heroes in their ideas of religion. Yet these three men seem to be one in death, not because they demonstrate our common mortality by dying, but because they do not quite die.

Each death resurrects a man his life forbade, single of soul and sure of his quest. Throughout *Daniel Deronda* Mordecai is too ill, too persecuted, and too poor to found his Zion; he longs only for a mystic brother in whom he may implant his vision. Only by dying can he infuse himself into his alter ego, Deronda, and begin the journey toward his thwarted dream. Dying, William Dorrit, like so many Victorians, is restored not to Zion, but to youth. Death frees him from the Marshalsea and the warped imagination it bred. He regains his soul when he regains his likeness to that paragon of integrity, his daughter. Death restores Heathcliff to full, triumphant demonism; his eyes, like the window that is the emblem of his soul's aspirations, need close no longer. In each scene a frustrated and fragmented man is renewed, not *beyond* death, but *in* it. He has found, at last, that treasure, that answer, that grace of stability and coherence, for which humanists have always yearned. Lionel Trilling dubs this stable core of identity "the own self."[6] It seems truer to the Victorian imagination to suggest that each man achieves when dying the vivid self-realization of the Victorian ghost, that spectacular epitome of the own self.

To thoughtful Victorians the self's extraordinariness was the beginning and the end. Religious consolations had become remote and incredible; in their capacity for revelation or perdition, lives became loci of holiness.[7] Points in the life cycle—childhood, conversion into maturity—seemed to promise an assurance of inward power, but this assurance dissolved at the moment it was grasped. Children proved elusive little actors, not touchstones of purity. Maturity was in theory the stable reward of a violent spiritual conversion into wholeness, but within this conversion fomented incessant, explosive mutation that refused to crystallize in noble adulthood. Theatricality—teasing, pyrotechnical, and self-creating—scattered the spirit's immutable majesty. Death was life's last great moment of change. Most of us imagine death as a negation, obliterating hope and consciousness forever, but Victorian death scenes embrace it as a final source of the integration lives promise and deny. If life cannot realize us, dying must, for there is nothing beyond.

This passion for death's cohering touch explains the embarrassing eroticism of so many Victorian deathbeds, especially those of women: Dickens' Little Nell, Emily Brontë's Catherine, Robert Browning's Pompilia, all become, in their lingering, lushly orchestrated deaths, aroused centers of desire. For all, the consummation that proved elusive in life explodes at life's end. The erotic female corpses, or near-corpses, with which so many Victorian paintings are decorated—Rossetti's *Beata Beatrix* and Millais's drowning Ophelia are orgiastically convulsed by death's approach—appear perverse or offensive in the necrophilic abandon they inspire.[8] However, they represent something more affirmative than a sinister fondness for dead women: these aroused corpses stimulate in the viewer the pride of life only death offers. They are not a perverse pocket of Victorian culture, but an expression of a common, if uncommonly powerful, cultural desire.

Mordecai, William Dorrit, and Heathcliff, the three dying men with which we began, all came to themselves in dying. The deaths of women arouse a desire and a fulfillment that are, in the same way, emblematic as well as erotic: at its end, the self surges forth in undivided intensity. Death in *East Lynne* comes "with a leap" to Isabel Vane, whose sin has been her abandonment to a medley of conflicting roles. Casting off the seemingly secure identities of lady, wife, and mother, she leaves her husband and children, playing the tragic narrative of the fallen woman until, maimed and disguised, she returns to her abandoned household in the role of self-effacing governess.

As we saw, her son Willie indicts her fragmentation by the purity, in his death scene, of his fixation on a single being—his lost "mamma"—but when Isabel confronts her own death shortly thereafter, the rift in her being is healed. Dying, she fulfills her marriage vows as she never did in life. Her death resanctifies her union with bigamous, befuddled Archibald Carlyle. In the novel's only scene of unabashed eroticism, she proclaims, as "Mr. Carlyle, with his own handkerchief, wipe[s] the death-dew from her forehead," "My sin will be remembered no more [in heaven] and we shall be together with our children for ever and for ever. Keep a little corner in your heart for poor lost Isabel." Garnished into "Think of me sometimes, keep one little corner in your heart for me—your poor—erring—lost Isabel!",[9] this prayer became the final line of T. A. Palmer's long-lived dramatization of Wood's novel, enticing generations of audiences to leave the theater with poor lost Isabel nesting in their hearts.[9]

But in the context of her dying plea (or is it a warning?), Mr. Carlyle would do well to keep more than a little corner available, for Isabel, his first wife, has just taken him away from his second, Barbara Hare, who has adored him single-mindedly throughout the novel. Isabel Vane's demise is her wedding night; the physicality of death gives her the power to arouse Mr. Carlyle to an ardor he has never shown. Not only does he wipe her death-dew with his own handkerchief; he seems to drink her death: "Lower and lower he bent his head, until his breath nearly mingled with hers"; "Mr. Carlyle laid her tenderly down again, and suffered his lips to rest upon hers."[10]

Death floods Lady Isabel with the self she has fractured: once more, she is "lady—wife—mother," and once more, if ghoulishly, Archibald Carlyle ratifies these roles by marrying her. As far as we see, neither God nor Christ forgives her, though she insists that they will; death alone seals her identity and restores "the own self." Dying, she orchestrates her own rebirth as liquidly seductive corpse, as irresistible ghost.

Emily Brontë, a loftier, less self-divided and sensuous woman, died nevertheless, according to her sister Charlotte's moving eulogy, with the same surge of being that animated the dying Isabel Vane. "Never in all her life had she lingered over any task that lay before her, and she did not linger now. She sank rapidly. She made haste to leave us. Yet while physically she perished, mentally, she grew stronger than we had yet known her. Day by day, when I saw with what a front she met suffering, I looked on her with an anguish of wonder and love. Stronger than a man, simpler than a child, her nature stood alone."[11]

The death of Emily Brontë is less teasingly erotic than Isabel Vane's, but it too consummates her integrity. She orchestrates her death as Isabel Vane does, though with pitilessness and epic resistance. Charlotte Brontë remembered and remade that death, a sisterly office Elizabeth Gaskell would perform in turn for her in *The Life of Charlotte Brontë*. Trying to redeem her friend from the charge of unwomanly coarseness, she makes her death scene the triumph of the exemplary woman the biography has affirmed all along.

As Gaskell presents it, Charlotte Brontë's life is a series of spectacular death scenes of which Charlotte is anguished spectator. Gaskell underplays the inevitable moment when Charlotte Brontë herself takes center stage by dying; this crowning death for which we have waited is a triumph of selflessness. Confronted, on her deathbed, with her new husband's "woe-worn face," Charlotte cries: "Oh! . . . I am not going to die, am I? He will not separate us, we have been so happy."[12] There is no agent in this cry, no "I" except a passionate suppliant who relinquishes herself to two powerful men: God (who is, in this biography, Death) and her husband. The Emily Brontë whom Charlotte had immortalized took on the solitary power of a personification of death. As Gaskell immortalizes Charlotte herself, she becomes, in her abandonment to death, the model of selflessness her biographer wants to consecrate. One sister is "stronger than a man," the other is womanhood perfected, but both Brontë sisters become types of the self-realization death brings the restless spirit.

These three blighted Victorian women, the fictional Isabel Vane and the legendary Brontë sisters, become, when touched with death, everything they could not be in life. Like Eliot's Mordecai, Dickens' William Dorrit, and Emily Brontë's own Heathcliff, but with an intense arousal heroes cannot emulate, these women crystallize their identities by dying. If in the midst of life, we are in death, Victorian iconography suggests that in the midst of death, we are also in life.

The vitality of our six corpses and their resurrections, not in a conventional afterlife, but during expiration, are both comforting and chilling. Like the apparently consecrated children whose beings exploded into pyrotechnical display, or the adults whose strenuous conversions threatened to go on erupting forever without progressing into perfected maturity, the Victorian dead cannot stop living. Conventional consolation shares its vision with Gothic horror; inspirational exemplars begin to sound like tales of terror. The surge of being that is death's endowment announces itself not only in deathbed redemptions, but in images of living death.

Like most nineteenth-century Gothic literature, Bram Stoker's *Dracula* plays on fears not of mortality but of immortality: death has no power over the undead, who prowl with hideously vigorous desire after the grave has closed over them. Vitality surges forth with vampirism, but is this unnatural life-in-death different from the vitality of death itself? Once she is vampirized, Stoker's pale, docile Lucy Westenra becomes a ravenous predator, ruddy with blood, whom the grave cannot subdue. But when Lucy becomes at last "true dead," in the fond phrase of her paternalistic killer, is her maiden corpse different in kind from the grinning, blood-glutted un-corpse of the undead?

> There, in the coffin lay no longer the foul Thing that we had so dreaded and grown to hate that the work of her destruction was yielded as a privilege to the one best entitled to it, but Lucy *as we had seen her in her life,* with her face of unequalled sweetness and purity. True that there were there, as we had seen them in life, the

traces of care and pain and waste; but these were all dear to us, for they marked her truth to what we knew. One and all we felt that the holy calm that lay like sunshine over the wasted face and form was only an earthly token and symbol of the calm that was to reign for ever.[13]

Undead, Lucy is a "foul Thing"; true dead, she is "Lucy as [they] had seen her in her life." Neither corpse is a corpse; both incarnate a living essence, of desire or docility.

In the nineteenth-century folk culture of actual death, the corpse acquires a similar magic, magnetic and quasi-alive. As Ruth Richardson describes it:

> A corpse has a presence of its own. It resembles the dead person, yet it is not that person. Death transforms the body of a known individual into something else—removing them from the realm of the ordinary in which survivors continue to have their being. . . . In the popular culture of the British Isles, as in that of many other peoples, death was believed to work some paradoxical magic—for after death the body possessed powers the living person never had, and commanded awe, even fear, when the living individual never may have done so.[14]

The horror of *Dracula* plays on the charisma of actual Victorian corpses and the futility of death's attempt to quench the theatrical lives of the self. Whether vampires walk or not, the dead do not die.

Dying well was an art, and the theater made the most of it. Sarah Bernhardt was especially famous for her death scenes. The notorious photograph of her sleeping in a coffin like a vampire welded her performing to her ordinary self. Onstage, her life was a pageant of vibrant deaths, which she continued to perform in the supposed privacy of sleep. In the 1890s Bernhardt's well-publicized rivalry with Eleonora Duse over the role of Marguerite Gauthier, the dying courtesan who is Dumas's *La Dame aux Camélias*, was really the theatrical triumph of death; on alternate nights the flamboyant Bernhardt and the austere Duse vied with each other as they died slowly, richly, carrying mesmerized audiences with them.

Men as well as women enthralled spectators by dying publicly. Henry Irving's first great success, in 1871, in Leopold Lewis' *The Bells*, was one bravura protracted death scene. Playing a respectable burgomaster who has murdered a Jewish traveler for his gold, Irving is confronted in a vision with accusing specters who, after tormenting him, hang him for his crime. At the end, half in his vision, half in domestic "reality," Irving mutters "in a voice of strangulation" his famous curtain line—"The rope! the rope! Take the rope from my neck!"—and dies.[15] When, as Mathias, his apparently impeccable life dissolved in guilt, Irving, like Bernhardt, turned himself into a worshiped angel of death.

Thirty-four years later, in 1905, Irving gained still more renown by dying as a saint. Ill and impoverished in the gloomy town of Bradford, he played the title role in Tennyson's *Becket*. His collapse in his hotel after the performance was obscured by the mystic resonance of his final onstage line: "into Thy hands, O Lord—into Thy hands." These words became so indelibly associated with the dead stage hero that Queen Alexandra herself inscribed them on the wreath she sent to Irving's pompous funeral in Westminster Abbey. Irving's public martyrdom in Tennyson's stately play allowed audiences to forget the seediness of his actual death. Dying as Tennyson's saint, not as a private man, Irving acted out the public, spectacular nature of all imagined death. Not only was dying never obscure, but, with Tennyson as its laureate, it was never real.

John Forster's *The Life of Charles Dickens* reluctantly grants its hero, who is cursed with the actor's inchoate energy, an actor's death. Forster's antitheatricalism makes that death less sacred than Irving's, but it is equally a triumph of self-creation. Dickens spends his final days in a frenzy of mad motion:

He had read the *Oliver Twist* scenes the night before at York; had just been able to get to the express train, after shortening the pauses in the reading, by a violent rush when it was over; and had travelled through the night. He appeared to me "dazed" and worn. No man could look more so than he did, that sorrowful morning. The end was near.[16]

The end comes, and in death as in life, Dickens is possessed by rival arts. Forster situates his tomb allegorically, doing his best to reconcile the author with the actor who, in his opinion, destroyed his hero: "The highest associations of both the arts he loved surround him where he lies. Next to him is RICHARD CUMBERLAND. MRS. PRITCHARD's monument looks down on him, and immediately behind is DAVID GARRICK's. Nor is the actor's delightful art more worthily represented than the nobler genius of the author. Facing the grave, and on its left and right, are the monuments of CHAUCER, SHAKESPEARE, and DRYDEN, the three immortals who did most to create and settle the language to which CHARLES DICKENS has given another undying name" (II, 418). Dead, Dickens joins a charmed community that allows him at last to be both author and actor. Bernhardt sleeping in her coffin, the satanic outsider Irving transmuted into Saint Thomas, Dickens crowned at last by the warring arts that ravaged his life— all commemorate death as the most consummately versatile of stage directors.

BECAUSE DEATH IS A STAR, nineteenth-century representations of lives are saturated in death. Children are consecrated less in themselves than for their presumptive affinity with death: they are more valuable as endings than origins. Charting the convulsions of maturity in *In Memoriam*, Tennyson prayed "that men may rise on stepping-stones / Of their dead selves to higher things." Dead selves fertilize growth and overshadow it. In the years of his greatest influence as Poet Laureate and seer, Tennyson became the national spokesman for death's seductive vagrancies. It was fitting that he had written the sonorous prayer transmuting Henry Irving into Saint Thomas Becket, for the intricate deaths he wrote about taught an empire how to die. King Arthur died regularly for Tennyson. In one of his many incarnations, Comyns Carr's 1895 adaptation of the revered *Idylls of the King,* Arthur became Henry Irving in his saintly guise. In its grandeur, its authority, and its ultimate failure, the passing of Tennyson's Arthur is the essence of all the deaths that have paraded by us.

King Arthur held a special place in the loved pageant of moribund culture heroes. To a triumphantly industrialized nation obsessed with its sins, he symbolized everything that had died in England's noble past. For Tennyson, he took on various personal incarnations—he was alternately the poet's own cherished Arthur Henry Hallam and his Queen's noble, lost Albert—but he was most effective as an epitome of the death of a nation. In "The Passing of Arthur," the last of the *Idylls of the King,* a deathly white mist swathes an England in which, it seems, only the mortally wounded Arthur and Sir Bedivere survive. "First made and latest left of all the knights," Sir Bedivere is the surviving spirit of the Round Table; he alone lives beyond the end of the epic. Overflowing with reverence, he is deficient in awe. Twice the stricken Arthur instructs Sir Bedivere to throw his magic sword, Excalibur, into the lake as a signal to its presiding female spirits that his mission is finished. Twice Sir Bedivere disobeys, on the ground that so rare an object should not be wasted on a desolate mere. As punishment, his life becomes a death, while the dying Arthur surges into life. When Sir Bedivere finally does throw the sword into the lake, he summons the supernatural company who will carry Arthur on his healing journey to Avilion. When they leave, the world goes out forever. The three queens who come for Arthur incarnate all life left and take it away with them:

> and from them rose
> A cry that shiver'd to the tingling stars,
> And, as it were one voice, an agony
> Of lamentation, like a wind that shrills
> All night in a waste land, where no one comes,
> Or hath come, since the making of the world.[17]

This one remaining voice sails with the dying king "beyond the limit of the world." Sir Bedivere, an unwilling custodian of civilization, is left alone in "the stillness of the dead world's winter dawn." When that winter evolves into spring, his world will not come to life, for Arthur has taken vitality to the island of the dead, whose welcoming cry Bedivere hears yearningly from his distant solitude.

"The Passing of Arthur" endows a king who has been ineffective throughout his epic with an authority he lacked in life. His stern command that Sir Bedivere throw Excalibur into the lake is his only injunction that is obeyed, and even this requires three iterations. Death gives Tennyson's blameless king a life he never lived.[18] Receding from a land he could not rule, King Arthur becomes, like Dracula, an undead creature, the vitality of whose protracted dying sucks life from the ordinary world. Death, not the king, is Tennyson's hero. When Arthur drains his empire by leaving it, he becomes its ruler at last.

Like all the works we have looked at, "The Passing of Arthur" is an elegy with a celebration in its heart. With envy and awe, it pays tribute to the superior energies of the dead. Sir Bedivere, the lone survivor in unutterable bleakness, is the true object of our mourning. In the spirit of Sir Bedivere straining, from lifeless silence, to hear the intense communal cries greeting Arthur, Victorian readers relished voyeuristic poetic intrusions on the feelings of the dead: surely, their intensity would galvanize poor survivors. Robert Browning's Bishop of St. Praxed rehearses his death with relish as a delicious drowning in the sensuous manifestations of religion: "And then how I shall lie through centuries, / And hear the blessed mutter of the Mass, / And see God made and eaten all day long, / And feel the steady candle-flame, and taste / Good strong thick stupefying incense-smoke!" ("The Bishop Orders his Tomb at St. Praxed's Church," ll. 80–84). The Bishop's Heaven is his earth; like King Arthur, he engorges the life of his world at last.

Gentler, more lyric death poems simulate dying in the hungry spirit of Browning's Bishop: wistfully, enviously, they stare at death, slide into it, and become the dead's consciousness. In none of these poems are the dead in heaven; in all, the dead engorge a life superior in intensity and fulfillment to that of the living. The surge of consummate being with which characters in novels die extends itself in poetry into a delicious living death.

In the spirit of Sarah Bernhardt in her coffin, female poets tend to play at death with an unself-conscious wit that Tennyson and Browning, or even Thomas Hardy in "Ah, Are You Digging on My Grave?," can only approximate, though the longing for an inward understanding of death is shared by women and men. The lilting rhythms of Christina Rossetti's "Song" ("When I am dead, my dearest") mask a reverie of power. Its second, concluding stanza sweetly affirms a corpse's privileges:

> I shall not see the shadows,
>  I shall not feel the rain;
> I shall not hear the nightingale
>  Sing on as if in pain.
> And dreaming through the twilight
>  That doth not rise or set,
> Haply I may remember,
>  And haply may forget.

> (ll. 9–16)

The surviving man seems paralyzed; it is the dead woman's prerogative to forget love, for only the dead can control their

dreams. In the same spirit and with the same sweetness, Emily
Brontë imagines death as a world remade:

> And if their eyes should watch and weep
> Till sorrow's source were dry,
> She would not, in her tranquil sleep,
> Return a single sigh.

> Blow, west wind, by the lonely mound,
> And murmur, summer streams,
> There is no need of other sound
> To soothe my Lady's dreams.[19]

In both poems the speaker imagines death lyrically, ironically,
as supreme self-possession. Life is not gone; it has simply become
controllable by the weaving, filtering, dreaming mind. Dying literary characters became the central actors of their stories; they
cast off the fragmentation that thwarted them in life. The dead
in Victorian poetry are not merely actors, but omnipotent stage
directors as well; they not only dominate their world, but order
it. In the nineteenth-century imagination, death gains stunning
power, even though it has lost the one power our own century has
learned to live with: it no longer kills.

The theatricality of Victorian death involves not only its primacy, its popularity, the burst of fulfillment it brings to character;
its vitalism also brings longevity, for its intensifications need
never end. As Garrett Stewart notes, Victorian death is not so
much an ending as a catastrophic—but still vital—transformation crowning a life cycle in which all transitions are transformations: "Death in nineteenth-century fiction becomes an em-
phatic way to name by metaphor or embody by alter ego certain
changes too violent and disjunctive for the alternative Romantic
metaphors of organic growth."[20] Refusing to conform to death's
limitations, the self makes dying a climax through which it dem-
onstrates and declares itself forever. In its self-creating flair, its
power to remake a scene, its perpetuity, the only being adequate

to the idea of Victorian death is the Victorian ghost, for the ghost embodies those intimations of potency the living dream of and fear.

In PERVERSE, quasi-occult fashion, Victorian literature echoes John Donne's triumphant battle cry; it too announces: "Death, thou shalt die." Its animated corpses, and more palpably, its ghosts and monsters, make death die as effectively as did the pantomime players who died and lived simultaneously;[21] the vitality within death dwarfs life itself. In the twentieth century haunting images of Auschwitz, Hiroshima, and Vietnam have abated Victorian awe at life's persistence; death comes not only easily, but collectively. We will not spring into ourselves on our deathbeds, but instead will become indistinguishable from the dying hordes whose images haunt our culture.

Our Gothic literature is arid, frightening us with the ease of death, not the tenacity of life. Alfred Hitchcock's classic nightmare *Psycho* shows viewers how easy it is to kill a heroine, leaving her story unfinished; moreover, she stays dead. Stephen King's vampires are not Bram Stoker's majestic undead, but the repulsive not-alive. The characterless creatures in King's *Salem's Lot* kill more effectively than did the florid Dracula, with his distracting telepathic play, his erotic hunger, and his dreams of empire, but they kill instinctively, without fun, individuality, or flair. Our Gothic images remind us that we are perishable, not only in ourselves, but as a species. Victorian monsters embody an awful immortality. Frankenstein's creature or Mr. Hyde or Dracula are horrible because they live when they shouldn't; we are horrible today because we die before we should.

Ghosts epitomize the powers of the Victorian dead. Like Victorian actors, they invade ordinary life with insistent visual intensity, becoming incarnations of unspoken faiths—in this case, faith in a self even death cannot contain or quench. In the nineteenth century ghosts are triumphs of "the insistent claims of the own self," as Lionel Trilling has called it, but they are neither single-minded nor sincere. They will not close their identities by dying, nor will they fix those identities in a sole self.

In Victorian England, Christmas was ghost season. A ritualistic culture, yearning feverishly for transcendence, possessed by faith but deprived of dogma, turned the occasion of the Savior's birth into a festival of weird apparitions: the infant Christ became another Victorian child the promise of whose beginnings was smothered by celebrations of death. Most Victorian ghost stories appeared in Christmas annuals.[22] Even writers free from publishers' rituals gravitated naturally to Christmas. M. R. James read his latest account of antiquarian specters regularly, every Christmas Eve, to a privileged circle of fellow members of the Chitchat Club.[23] Thomas Hardy's nostalgic poem "Yuletide in a Younger World" associates his lost, authentic, Christmas-Eve, not with salvation, but with specters:

We had eyes for phantoms then,
    And at bridge or stile
        On Christmas Eve
Clear beheld those countless ones who had crossed it
        Cross again in file:—
Such has ceased longwhile![24]

Christmas, the gargantuan festival that to many of us epitomizes Victorian England, was less the occasion of the Incarnation than the release of the spectral, the mutant, the bizarre. It was the season of pantomime as well as ghosts, that phantasmagoria of hybrid lives and ritual transformations. After 1904, it became the season of *Peter Pan,* whose pageant of boys who are not boys, pirate-fathers, little girls playing ideal mothers, fairies who exist only when we applaud, combined the spectacular metamorphoses of pantomime with ghosts' irresistible visual demand that we believe in them. By 1916 Lord Dunsany could write with assurance, in "Thirteen at Table," that Christmas is the season not of miracles, but of spooks. The story begins: "In front of a spacious fire-place of the old kind, when the logs were well alight, and men with pipes and glasses were gathered before it in great easeful chairs, and the wild weather outside and the comfort that was within, and the season of the year—for it was Christmas—and the hour of the night, all called for the weird or uncanny, then out spoke the ex-master of fox-hounds and told this tale."[25]

Even *A Christmas Carol,* that tribute to Victorian faith in con-version if not in God, is a ghost story before it is anything else. Scrooge "keeps Christmas" by seeing ghosts and believing in them more than he does in his life. Marley's ghost, like all the dead we have seen, is the living man made manifest: "The same face: the very same. Marley in his pig-tail, usual waistcoat, tights, and boots; the tassels on the latter bristling, like his pig-tail, and his coat-skirts, and the hair upon his head. The chain he drew was clasped about his middle. It was long, and wound about him like a tail; and it was made (for Scrooge observed it closely) of cash-boxes, keys, padlocks, ledgers, deeds, and heavy purses wrought in steel."[26]

Under the tutelage of ghosts, Scrooge becomes an ideal audi-ence. Like a child at a pantomime, he watches in wonder the spectacle of his own past, then laughs, weeps, and exclaims as the families of his nephew Fred and the Cratchits perform their lives for him. By the end he commemorates Christmas by becom-ing a ghost himself. Like the spirits who convert him out of soli-tude, Scrooge in his benevolence turns into a spectacle of Lon-don. Having become "as good a friend, as good a master, and as good a man, as the good old city knew," he is ready to join the dead.

Death in *A Christmas Carol* transfigures ordinary life by up-staging it. Like Christmas, ghost stories bring promises of immor-tality, apparent assurances that death will die, but the salvation they promise is unrecognizable by orthodox criteria. Their con-solation assures us only that the advent of death, which Dickens figures as the coming of ghosts, brings a self-realization so intense that normalcy cannot contain it.

In a sense, Scrooge joins his tutelary ghosts at the end of his story. In this spirit, the best nineteenth-century ghosts insinuate themselves into their spectator, so that ghost and ghost-seer manifest themselves as one single terrible being. Oliver Onions' magnificent twentieth-century tale "The Beckoning Fair One" (1911), whose thwarted novelist becomes indistinguishable from the phantom he pursues or who is pursuing him, is a parable of all Victorian visitations. Jack Sullivan defines its symbiotic merging of identities between spectator and specter: "The Beckoning Fair One represents the final triumph of the imagination, the subjective fusion of 'joy' and 'terror'; neither can be separated from the other, for both belong to the unified 'category of absolute things.' When the narrator submits to The Beckoning Fair One, he also, unfortunately, submits to the loss of his sanity, becoming, as much as the expected other ghost, a deranged spectre who lowers all the blinds and haunts his own house (much as Brydon later does in Henry James's 'The Jolly Corner')."[27]

In 1890 Vernon Lee defined, in *Hauntings*, these "spurious ghosts" who manifest themselves by claiming certain malleable identities: "My ghosts are what you call spurious ghosts (according to me the only genuine ones), of whom I can affirm only one thing, that they haunted certain brains, and have haunted, among others, my own and my friends."[28] In a series of supernatural tales dominated by "spurious ghosts" that are the most vivid presences in their tales, Victorian ghost-seers exalt and destroy themselves by turning into the preternatural beings they see.

Wilkie Collins' "The Dream Woman," Henry James's *The Turn of the Screw,* and Vernon Lee's "A Phantom Lover" give us supernatural visitants who invade the identities of their prey. Collins' "she-devil," with flaxen hair, delicate white arms with down on them, a drooping left eyelid, and an upraised knife, has external existence in her tale, but she is most effective as a terrible apparition in her husband's recurrent dream. James's Peter Quint and Miss Jessel have lived and died independently of the governess' consciousness; they invade that consciousness to become the woman they terrify. Alice Oke, the seventeenth-century murderer who, in "A Phantom Lover," takes over the identity of the modern Mrs. Oke, lived and died two centuries before Lee's story begins. These revenants do not need the lives of those they haunt; artfully, they remake those lives in their own images. Their power teeters ambiguously between the supernatural and the psychological. James's fidelity to the Victorian ghost story, not his sophisticated Modernism, explains the imperceptible boundary between fact and vision as the governess capitulates to the ghosts. Wilkie Collins, Henry James, and Vernon Lee are concerned less with the objective existence of the supernatural than they are with the porous potential of identity. Their ghosts dramatize a power in which all Victorian writers believed, that of the superior integrity of the dead.

In "The Dream Woman" (1859) a prophetic dream takes on the ghost's visual irresistibility and power to transform. On his birthday, Isaac Scratchard dreams of a deceptively delicate woman plunging a knife into his own sleeping form. Some time later, he meets this woman and, under a strange compulsion, marries her. They hate each other and separate; the dream recurs relentlessly. We expect waking and sleeping life to converge in the murder so heavily predicted, but the obvious ending never comes. We leave Isaac lost in the dream that has become his life. Literal prophecy is not Collins' subject: his quasi-ghost story commemorates the accelerating vitality of death. Isaac dreams— and will presumably be killed—at the hour of his birth. The death he watches over and over is stronger than that birth, just as his ghostly dream is stronger than his waking life.

Like *A Christmas Carol*, "The Dream Woman" pays tribute to the primacy of ghosts. In both, spectral intruders do not mimic life, but dictate it; death is an incessant shaper of a life that fades at its touch. Acting itself over and over, Isaac's death gives his nonlife the only vitality and meaning it knows; ghostly visitations galvanize Scrooge into an emotional and moral arousal that countinghouse, family, and city cannot provide. With the same irrepressibility, death brought meaning and glory to the lives of such mythic heroes as Henry Irving or King Arthur.

Henry James's *The Turn of the Screw* (1898) is as implacable as Collins' more modest tale in its eminently Victorian insistence on the power of ghosts—and the vibrant power of the dead they represent—over the fragmented minds of the living. In "The Dream Woman," Isaac's actual murder, if it ever takes place, is an anticlimax beyond the interest of the story; the objective validity of the ghostly dream matters less than its power to shape the dreamer. In *The Turn of the Screw* the actual presence of Peter Quint and Miss Jessel at Bly, where they may or may not possess the children they have already formed in any case, matters less than does the superiority of their lives to that of the governess they haunt. As with Collins' Dream Woman, or Oliver Onions' Beckoning Fair One, the ghosts bring the only elation life offers her; it is they who make the children "interesting." Her first, vivid sight of Peter Quint is of a man who "gives me a sort of sense of looking like an actor." Like those of Oscar Wilde's histrionic Canterville Ghost, Peter Quint's bravura self-presentations remind us that all Victorian ghosts are actors in their obsession with their own visibility. When the governess determines that Quint is a ghost, with a ghostly mistress, her suppressed existence is charged with the joy of performance. Even the gloomy Bly becomes taut with theatricality:

> The summer had turned, the summer had gone; the autumn had dropped upon Bly, and had blown out half our lights. The place, with its grey sky and withered garlands, its bared spaces and scattered dead leaves, was like a theatre after the performance—all strewn with crumpled playbills. There were exactly states of the air, conditions of sound and of stillness, unspeakable impressions

of the *kind* of ministering moment, that brought back to me, long
enough to catch it, the feeling of the medium in which, that June
evening out of doors, I had had my first sight of Quint, and in
which too, at those other instants, I had, after seeing him through
the window, looked for him in vain in the circle of the shrub-
bery.[29]

The "medium" in which the governess saw and then searched
for Quint is not so much the spring weather as the theater with
which he has galvanized her life. The actor-ish Quint and his
stagily weeping partner Miss Jessel bring to a starved life the gifts
of all Victorian ghosts: the vibrancy, the momentary transformations, the heightened, crystallized energy, of the stage. They play
the same role as does the pageant of the vital dying and dead with
which we began. They are signs of death's power to realize the
self, and also of death's powerlessness to kill. The theatricality
with which they transform a dull household both answers pious
prayers and laughs at them.

Vernon Lee was herself the dashing theatrical persona of Violet
Paget. Perhaps because Paget invented her own authorial self, her
ghosts are more overtly erotic, theatrical, and invigorating intruders on dreary life than are those of Collins and James. They
may be evil, but no one in the tales doubts that life would be
desolate without them. In this they epitomize the qualities of the
dead that glorify even the most mundane and duty-bound of Victorian lives: they bring mightiness to the self thirsting for might.

In Lee's "A Phantom Lover" (1886) the bored wife of a stolid
landowner, Mr. Oke of Okehurst (who is also her cousin), ani-
mates her listless existence by transforming it, little by little, into
a work of art. The medium she chooses is her namesake, Alice
Oke, who in the seventeenth century scandalized the family by
betraying her own stolid husband with a lover and then, disguised
as a boy, murdering that lover for the highest of romantic mo-
tives.

As in "The Dream Woman" and *The Turn of the Screw,* the

literalness of the wicked Alice Oke's manifestation proves unimportant. What matters is her heightened life, which the reader as well as the heroine comes to desire. In the course of the story the living Alice Oke haunts the other characters by becoming the dead woman who haunts her, leading the artist-narrator to brood on spectral power. As he celebrates them, ghosts bring neither corruption nor salvation, but glorification of the sort Jane Eyre realized when she too was touched by the dead:

> We have all heard of ghosts, had uncles, cousins, grandmothers, nurses, who have seen them; we are all a bit afraid of them at the bottom of our soul; so why shouldn't they be? I am too skeptical to believe in the impossibility of anything, for my part! Besides, when a man has lived throughout a summer in the same house with a woman like Mrs. Oke of Okehurst, he gets to believe in the possibility of a great many improbable things, I assure you, as a mere result of believing in her. And when you come to think of it, why not? That a weird creature, visibly not of this earth, a reincarnation of a woman who murdered her lover two centuries and a half ago, that such a creature should have the power of attracting about her (being altogether superior to earthly lovers) the man who loved her in a previous existence, whose love for her was death—what is there astonishing in that?[30]

The narrator stands rapt before a fusion of the living and the spectral Alice Oke, who have become one weird, and utterly victorious, creature. In this characteristic moment in Vernon Lee's supernatural tales—it recurs in "Prince Alberic and the Snake Lady" and "Amour Dure"—a male narrator is enthralled by a woman whose life devours centuries, and who embodies all the transfiguring possibilities of intercourse with the dead. Her alliance with death offers the most compelling life the storyteller can imagine.

THE PERVERSITY OF VERNON LEE'S "Phantom Lover" differs only in its emphasis from the stately deaths of George Eliot's prophet

Mordecai, or Tennyson's King Arthur. For all, death brings the energy of identity that living thwarts. The noble novel, the sonorous national epic, and the tale of terror spring from a common source: a yearning for glory ordinary life cannot fathom. Only death brings the self into its inheritance, one so mighty it cannot be killed. Bearing a legacy of potential grandeur like that which determines the Victorian life cycle, the living stagger, but the dead walk.

## · EPILOGUE ·

## *Theatrical Fears*

One night, while writing about Henry Irving, Gordon Craig, that rebellious child of Victorian theatrical aestheticism, saw a ghost, or said he did. He describes his ghost with characteristic Hamlet-like flourishes:

> You must not think I exaggerate. I was alone—the wind, 'tis true, was howling down the valley outside my house—how it howwwled!—yet all was cosy and well lit in my room—nothing dusky, nothing weird: yet there—there stood Irving.
> Perhaps you have never seen a spirit. It is impossible for me to pass a week without seeing one—but then, I make no effort to raise a spirit—one is there—or there—and here was Irving . . . a kind of apparition—yes, that was it—and a kind voice saying, "Well, my boy, fiddling with a pen—what?" [1]

Unlike the real Irving, this apparition is benign. He points out the ways in which the modern theater has gone astray, and says that Gordon Craig himself is wonderful and a leader. Like Hamlet's father, he is a visual emblem of an unfinished mission, but he does not howl with the wind. He is cozily paternalistic, agreeing obligingly with whatever crochet Craig the ghost-seer puts forth.

Though he has mellowed, this apparitional Irving, like so many Victorian specters, blends ghost and actor in one image. He is the last, perhaps the only, actor-ghost to be seen in this century. By 1930 his appearance is consoling rather than frightening, but it raises haunting memories of the century in which Irving did howl and frighten people. The ghost Gordon Craig welcomes into his study is a faint image from a culture whose actors were menacing presences, transmitting radical threats to knowable identity.

As we have seen, the actor is one image of the Victorian anti-self, capering and mocking sincere emotion. The actor is associated too with the bestial, with monstrous, vampiristic, and spectral mutations. Though some of the most beloved performers and, at least in the first half of the century, some of the most innovative theatrical managers were women, proper women were shielded (and often shielded themselves) from the public transmutations of the theater.[2] Performers gave their lives to amuse, only to confront intense, half-acknowledged cultural fears.

The Victorian theater did not court the mistrust that surrounded and perhaps even energized it. Most theater historians congratulate its steady rise, during the course of the nineteenth century, to recognizability and respectability.[3] By the end of the century actors, at least the most prominent of them, were doing their best to prove that they were flesh-and-blood professionals of ordinary stature, not howling visitants from an unknown sphere who threatened everything middle-class citizens thought of as natural. They wanted only to seem recognizably human. Is it possible to locate the cause of the anxiety that the theatrical institution worked strenuously to pacify?

I suggest that the source of Victorian fears of performance lay not on the stage, but in the histrionic artifice of ordinary life. Playing themselves continually, convinced of the spiritual import of their lives, Victorian men and women validated those lives with the sanction of nature but feared that nature was whatever the volatile self wanted it to be. The theater was a visible reminder of the potential of good men and women to undergo inexplicable changes. Its menace was not its threat to the integrity of sincerity, but the theatricality of sincerity itself. The specter that audiences called the actor performed lives they recognized as their own.

8:00 p.m.

20 June 83

Denver - 2nd Show def 1

*Notes*

*Index*

# · NOTES ·

## Introduction: Trees and Transfigurations

1. Thomas Carlyle, "Biography" (1832); rpt. *Critical and Miscellaneous Essays,* 5 vols. (New York: AMS Press, 1969), III, 52.
2. John Henry Newman, *Apologia Pro Vita Sua* (1864; rpt. New York: W. W. Norton, 1968), p. 12.
3. Thomas Carlyle, *On Heroes, Hero-Worship and the Heroic in History* (1840), in *Sartor Resartus* and *On Heroes and Hero Worship* (rpt. London: J. M. Dent, 1967), p. 340. Future references to this edition will appear in the text, abbreviated as *HHW.*
4. David Friedrich Strauss, *The Life of Jesus, Critically Examined,* trans. Mary Ann Evans, 3 vols. (London: Chapman Brothers, 1846), III, 425–426.
5. George Eliot, *Middlemarch* (1871–72; rpt. New York: W. W. Norton, 1977), p. xiv.
6. *Ellen Terry's Memoirs,* with Preface, Notes, and Additional Biographical Material by Edith Craig and Christopher St. John (1932; rpt. New York: Benjamin Blom, 1969), p. 304.
7. Oscar Wilde, *The Picture of Dorian Gray* (1891; rpt. Middlesex: Penguin Books, 1949), pp. 158–159.
8. Erving Goffman, *The Presentation of Self in Everyday Life* (Garden City, N.Y.: Anchor Books, 1959), p. 235.
9. Lionel Trilling, *Sincerity and Authenticity* (Cambridge, Mass.: Harvard University Press, 1972), p. 73. Trilling has not had the last word. His phobia about theatricality, among other things, has made him a marginal figure to a deconstructing scholarly generation that aims to make sacred truths dissolve. In *A Future for Astyanax: Character and Desire in Literature* (New York: Little, Brown, 1976), for instance, Leo Bersani is a passionate advocate of the "theatricalized" self that deconstructs the nineteenth-century myth of ontological continuity and coherence. Like Oscar Wilde, though, Bersani locates his exploding, theatrical selves in the realm of the literarily and theatrically perverse; in the British Victorian canon, they are

barely perceptible. I am arguing that even at the seemingly stable core of nineteenth-century belief—the universal authenticity of lives as writers imagine them—the self is a carrier of theatrical disorder. Though it does not mention the theater, Jacob Korg's "The Rage of Caliban," *University of Toronto Quarterly* 37 (October 1967): 75–89, is an excellent survey of the confusion in canonical Victorian literature between integral, double, and multiple selves.

10. Jonas Barish, *The Antitheatrical Prejudice* (Berkeley and London: University of California Press, 1981), p. 76.

11. See Terry Castle, *Masquerade and Civilization: The Carnivalesque in Eighteenth-Century English Culture and Fiction* (Stanford: Stanford University Press, 1986), p. 253: "This realm of dream, dismay, and laughter is also, par excellence, the realm of women." Castle discusses only the masquerade, an antisocial interlude that disrupted only temporarily the certainties of eighteenth-century British culture. In the nineteenth century, as I see it, the principle of masquerade—especially its imagination of endless "unnatural" inversions and transformations that undermine identities we think we know—mutates into theatricality, becoming, not a carnival interlude, but a central, if fearful, mode of perceiving daily reality. Insofar as the articles of faith it makes dissolve are patriarchal, this spirit of play is perceived by patriarchal culture as demonically female.

12. Drama critic, playwright, and author of *On Actors and the Art of Acting*—an art to which no previous Victorian had paid public tribute—George Henry Lewes discerned and encouraged the actress lurking in Mary Ann Evans, without whom George Eliot may not have been able to write at all. For more on the theatricality of their partnership, see Nina Auerbach, "Secret Performances: George Eliot and the Art of Acting," in *Romantic Imprisonment: Women and Other Glorified Outcasts* (New York: Columbia University Press, 1986), pp. 253–267.

13. For a definitive account of the dynamic collaboration between Victorian painting and theater, see Martin Meisel, *Realizations: Narrative, Pictorial, Theatrical Arts in Nineteenth-Century England* (Princeton: Princeton University Press, 1983).

14. Quoted in *English Plays of the Nineteenth Century: Pantomimes, Extravaganzas and Burlesques*, ed. Michael R. Booth (Oxford: Clarendon Press, 1976), p. 486.

15. Reprinted in Charles Dickens, *Christmas Books, and Reprinted Pieces* (New York: John Wurtele Lovell, n.d.), p. 832. For a striking analysis of the grasp of pantomime on Dickens' literary imagination, see Edwin M. Eigner, *The Dickens Pantomime* (Berkeley, Los Angeles, and London: University of California Press, 1989).

16. A. E. Wilson, *King Panto: The Story of Pantomime* (New York: E. P. Dutton & Co., 1935), p. 159.
17. *Plays by H. J. Byron*, ed. Jim Davis (Cambridge: Cambridge University Press, 1984), p. 74.
18. Michael R. Booth, *Prefaces to English Nineteenth-Century Theatre*, 5 vols. (Manchester: Manchester University Press, [1969–1976]), p. 25.
19. For a description, see Terry Castle, "Phantasmagoria: Spectral Technology and the Metaphorics of Modern Reverie," *Critical Inquiry* 15 (Autumn 1988): 26–61.

## I. Little Actors

1. Ellen Wood, *East Lynne* (1861; rpt. New Jersey: Rutgers University Press, 1984), p. 484. Future references to this edition will appear in the text.
2. T. A. Palmer, *East Lynne*, in *Nineteenth-Century British Drama*, ed. Leonard R. N. Ashley (1874; rpt. Glenview, Ill.: Scott, Foresman and Co., 1967), p. 390.
3. Charlotte Brontë, *Jane Eyre* (1847; rpt. Middlesex: Penguin Books, 1966), p. 99. Future references to this edition will appear in the text, abbreviated as *JE*.
4. Charles Dickens, *The Old Curiosity Shop* (1841; rpt. Middlesex: Penguin Books, 1972), pp. 508–509.
5. Emily Brontë, *Wuthering Heights* (1847; rpt. Middlesex: Penguin Books, 1965), p. 61.
6. Charles Dickens, *Great Expectations* (1860–61; rpt. Middlesex: Penguin Books, 1963), pp. 35–36.
7. Jerome Hamilton Buckley, *Season of Youth: The Bildungsroman from Dickens to Golding* (Cambridge, Mass.: Harvard University Press, 1974), p. 18; *The Voyage In: Fictions of Female Development*, ed. Elizabeth Abel, Marianne Hirsch, and Elizabeth Langland (Hanover, N.H.: University Press of New England, 1983). For a similar inward-looking, expansion-denying title, see *The Private Self: Theory and Practice of Women's Autobiographical Writings*, ed. Shari Benstock (Chapel Hill and London: University of North Carolina Press, 1988).
8. George Eliot, *The Mill on the Floss* (1860; rpt. Middlesex: Penguin Books, 1979), p. 65.
9. Philippe Ariès, *Centuries of Childhood: A Social History of Family Life*, trans. Robert Baldick (1960; rpt. New York: Vintage Books, 1962), p. 32.
10. Many social scientists today give children the authority to tell adults who they are; Carol Gilligan is one of the most influential. *In a Different Voice: Psychological Theory and Women's Development* (Cambridge, Mass.: Har-

vard University Press, 1982) examines the separate psychic identities of boys and girls as a guide to separations she perceives among adults. Gilligan relies on gender stereotypes as absolute as any dictated by the Victorians; on pp. 130–32 she uses George Eliot's Maggie to support her vision of female altruism victimized by "male" moral abstractions. Elsewhere, Gilligan defines with the same rigidity the female "activity of friend-making [in contrast to] the boys' portrayal of a self bounded in separation." Carol Gilligan, "The Conquistador and the Dark Continent: Reflections on the Psychology of Love," *Daedalus: Journal of the American Academy of Arts and Sciences* 113 (Summer 1984): 92. As in Victorian mythmaking, Gilligan's rigid gender distinctions make the child the vehicle of adult needs to affirm singleness of being.

11. Thomas Carlyle, *Sartor Resartus* (1833; rpt. London: J. M. Dent & Sons, 1967), p. 82.

12. Martin Meisel, *Realizations: Narrative, Pictorial, and Theatrical Arts in Nineteenth-Century England* (Princeton: Princeton University Press, 1983), p. 30. Meisel, pp. 39–51, defines pictorial theater economically and definitively.

13. John Stokes, Michael R. Booth, and Susan Bassnett, *Bernhardt, Terry, Duse: The Actress in her Time* (Cambridge: Cambridge University Press, 1988), p. 4.

14. Tom Robertson, *Caste, The Principal Dramatic Works of Thomas William Robertson*, 2 vols. (London: Sampson Low, Marston, Searle & Rivington, 1889), pp. 122, 145.

15. For lucid descriptions of the gorgeous nonsense motivating the transformations of the pantomime "plot," see Meisel, *Realizations*, p. 184, and Edwin M. Eigner, *The Dickens Pantomime* (Berkeley and Los Angeles: University of California Press, 1989), pp. 41–45.

16. For Jean Davenport and the Infant Phenomenon, see Eric Wollencott Barnes, *The Lady of Fashion: The Life and Times of Anna Cora Mowatt* (New York: Charles Scribner's Sons, 1954), p. 246. For an account of Ben Terry's theatrical dynasty, which continues through the twentieth century in the work of Gordon Craig, Edith Craig, and John Gielgud, see Nina Auerbach, *Ellen Terry, Player in Her Time* (New York: W. W. Norton, 1987).

17. Elizabeth Gaskell, *The Life of Charlotte Brontë* (1857; rpt. Middlesex: Penguin Books, 1975), p. 84. Future references to this edition will appear in the text.

18. Oscar Wilde, "The Critic as Artist," *Plays, Prose Writings, and Poems* (1890; rpt. London: J. M. Dent & Sons, 1978), p. 48.

19. Alexander Welsh's *From Copyright to Copperfield: The Identity of Dickens* (Cambridge, Mass.: Harvard University Press, 1987) is a stimulating ex-

ception to the assumption that the adult Dickens was made by the deprived child. Welsh speculates that a middle-aged Dickens, whose sense of his own integrity was shaken, created the suffering child of the autobiographical fragment as an antidote to his growing bad faith.

20. John Forster, *The Life of Charles Dickens*, 2 vols. (1872–1874; rpt. London: J. M. Dent & Sons, Everyman's Library, 1948), I, 12–13. Future references to this edition will appear in the text.

21. *The Collected Ghost Stories of Mrs. J. H. Riddell*, ed. E. F. Bleiler (New York: Dover Publications, 1977), p. 156.

22. M. R. James, *Ghost Stories of an Antiquary*, ed. E. F. Bleiler (1904; rpt. New York: Dover Books, 1971), pp. 33–34.

23. Henry James, *The Turn of the Screw* (1898; rpt. New York: W. W. Norton, 1966), p. 39.

24. J. M. Barrie, *Peter Pan* (1911; rpt. New York: Bantam Classics, 1985), p. 163.

25. J. M. Barrie, *Peter Pan* (1928; rpt. *Peter Pan and Other Plays*, New York: AMS Press, 1975), act V, scene 2, p. 145. Future references to this edition will appear in the text.

26. J. M. Barrie, *A Well-Remembered Voice*, in *Peter Pan and Other Plays* (New York: AMS Press, 1975), pp. 204–205.

27. Denis Mackail, *Barrie: The Story of J. M. B.* (New York: Charles Scribner's Sons, 1941), p. 347.

28. J. M. Barrie, *The Little White Bird: Or Adventures in Kensington Gardens* (1902; rpt. New York: Charles Scribner's Sons, 1927), p. 158. Future references to this edition will appear in the text.

## II. Patterns of Conversion

1. Alfred Lord Tennyson, *In Memoriam*, I, 1–5 (1850; rpt. New York: W. W. Norton, 1973), p. 4. Future references to this edition will appear in the text.

2. Jerome Hamilton Buckley, *The Victorian Temper: A Study in Literary Culture* (1951; rpt. Cambridge, Mass.: Harvard University Press, 1969), pp. 91–92. Future references to Buckley will appear in the text.

3. Thomas Carlyle, *On Heroes, Hero-Worship and the Heroic in History* (1840), in *Sartor Resartus* and *On Heroes and Hero Worship* (rpt. London: J. M. Dent, 1967), p. 449–450. Future references to this edition will appear in the text, abbreviated as *HHW*.

4. George Levine, *Darwin and the Novelists: Patterns of Science in Victorian Fiction* (Cambridge, Mass., and London: Harvard University Press, 1988), p. 239.

5. August 1838. Quoted in Gillian Beer, *Darwin's Plots: Evolutionary Narra-*

*tive in Darwin, George Eliot and Nineteenth-Century Fiction* (London and Boston: Routledge & Kegan Paul, 1983), pp. 15, 29. Future references to Beer will appear in the text.

6. Quoted in Michael R. Booth, *Prefaces to English Nineteenth-Century Theatre* (Manchester: Manchester University Press, 1969–1976), pp. 167–168.

7. Terry Castle, *Masquerade and Civilization: The Carnivalesque in Eighteenth-Century English Culture and Fiction* (Stanford: Stanford University Press, 1986), p. 53.

8. See David J. DeLaura, "Ruskin, Arnold, and Browning's Grammarian: 'Crowded with Culture,'" in *Victorian Perspectives: Six Essays*, ed. John Clubbe and Jerome Meckier (London: Macmillan Press, 1989), p. 85.

9. David Marshall, *The Figure of Theater: Shaftesbury, Defoe, Adam Smith, and George Eliot* (New York: Columbia University Press, 1986), p. 128.

10. Jonas Barish, *The Antitheatrical Prejudice* (Berkeley and London: University of California Press, 1981), pp. 105–106.

11. Charles Dickens, *David Copperfield* (1849–50; rpt. Middlesex: Penguin Books, 1966), pp. 916, 938. Future references to this edition will appear in the text.

12. Oliver Onions, *The First Book of Ghost Stories: Widdershins* (1911; rpt. New York: Dover Publications, 1971), p. 151.

13. *Engaged*, act II, *Plays by W. S. Gilbert*, ed. George Rowell (Cambridge: Cambridge University Press, 1982), p. 152; my italics.

14. Quoted in Cecil Woodham-Smith, *Florence Nightingale: 1820–1910* (New York and London: McGraw-Hill, 1951), p. 67.

15. Elizabeth Gaskell, *North and South* (1854–55; rpt. Middlesex: Penguin English Library, 1970), p. 508. Future references to this edition will appear in the text. Although I discuss only *North and South* here, similar interludes recur in novels by Victorian women; George Eliot's *Romola* and Charlotte Brontë's *Jane Eyre* come to mind. In all, if only briefly, the female protagonist is "converted" away from external authority to rely on her own conscience. This interlude is generally dissociated from the novel's plot. In this it resembles a theatrical *tableau vivant*, whose autonomous ingenuity or power is its own aesthetic reward.

16. *Ellen Terry's Memoirs*, with Preface, Notes, and Additional Biographical Material by Edith Craig and Christopher St. John (1932; rpt. New York: Benjamin Blom, 1969), pp. 86–87.

17. For more on the mingled power and capitulation of Ellen Terry's moment of conquest, see Nina Auerbach, *Ellen Terry, Player in Her Time* (New York: W. W. Norton, 1987), pp. 171–174.

18. Catherine Gallagher reads this scene ironically: the general shock at Margaret's sexual boldness in rushing to Thornton indicates the impossibility

of women exerting any public, political power directly; see *The Industrial Reformation of English Fiction: Social Discourse and Narrative Form, 1832–1876* (Chicago: University of Chicago Press, 1985), p. 173. Margaret's *theatrical* power, however, has an indelible intensity beyond the subsidence her plot requires. Barbara Harman writes shrewdly about the political connotations of Margaret's rush into the streets, claiming that *North and South* grows out of a widespread debate about women's right to a public identity. Like Gallagher and most other critics, however, Harman dwells exclusively on the sexual implications of Margaret's self-exposure, ignoring its theatrical component; see Barbara Leah Harman, "In Promiscuous Company: Female Public Appearance in Elizabeth Gaskell's *North and South,*" *Victorian Studies* 31 (Spring 1988): 351–374.

19. Elizabeth Gaskell, "The Poor Clare" (1858), in *The Works of Mrs. Gaskell,* 8 vols. (rpt. New York: AMS Press; New York: G. P. Putnam's Sons, 1906), V, 362; my italics.

20. Elizabeth Gaskell, *The Life of Charlotte Brontë* (1857; rpt. Middlesex: Penguin Books, 1975), p. 259. Future references to this edition will appear in the text.

21. John Forster, *The Life of Charles Dickens,* 2 vols. (1872–1874; rpt. London: J. M. Dent & Sons, Everyman's Library, 1948), I, 45–46. Future references to this edition will appear in the text.

22. Frances Donaldson, *The Actor-Managers* (Chicago: Henry Regnery Co., 1970), p. 51. Future references to this edition will appear in the text.

23. Quoted in Marius Goring. "Foreword," *Henry Irving and The Bells,* ed. David Mayer (Manchester: Manchester University Press, 1980), p. xv.

24. Bram Stoker, *Personal Reminiscences of Henry Irving,* 2 vols. (New York and London: The Macmillan Co., 1906), I, 242–245, 273.

25. Bram Stoker, *Dracula* (1897; rpt. New York: Bantam Classics, 1981), p. 35; final ellipsis Stoker's.

26. For a full account of the fearful power of female mutation over the Victorian imagination, see Nina Auerbach, *Woman and the Demon: The Life of a Victorian Myth* (Cambridge, Mass.: Harvard University Press, 1982).

27. Cary M. Mazer, "Male Jekyll, Female Hyde: Victorian Acting Theory, Gender, and the Divided Self," unpublished paper delivered at the University of Washington, 1989, ms. pp. 9–10.

28. There have been many rich studies of the Victorian female invalid in the past few decades. See especially Barbara Ehrenreich and Deirdre English, *For Her Own Good: 150 Years of the Experts' Advice to Women* (Garden City, N.Y.: Anchor Press, 1978); Jean Strouse, *Alice James: A Biography* (New York: Bantam Books, 1980); Elaine Showalter, *The Female Malady: Women, Madness, and English Culture, 1830–1980* (New York: Pantheon Books, 1985); Carroll Smith-Rosenberg, "The Hysterical Woman: Sex

Roles and Role Conflict in Nineteenth-Century America," in *Disorderly Conduct: Visions of Gender in Victorian America* (New York: Alfred A. Knopf, 1985), pp. 197–216; and Athena Vrettos, "In Sickness and in Health: Victorian Fictions of Disease," unpub. diss., University of Pennsylvania, 1988.

29. For detailed accounts of Charcot's clinic and extraordinary photographs of his patients, see George Frederick Drinka, *Myth, Malady and the Victorians* (New York: Simon and Schuster, 1984), and Showalter, *Female Malady*, pp. 148–154. Future references to Drinka's book will appear in the text.

## III. Death Scenes

1. J. M. Barrie, *Peter Pan* (1928; rpt. *Peter Pan and Other Plays*, New York: AMS Press, 1975), act III, p. 94.
2. Philippe Ariès, *The Hour of Our Death*, trans. Helen Weaver (New York: Alfred A. Knopf, 1981), p. 293.
3. George Eliot, *Daniel Deronda* (1876; rpt. Middlesex: Penguin Books, 1967), p. 882.
4. Charles Dickens, *Little Dorrit* (1857; rpt. Middlesex: Penguin Books, 1967), p. 712.
5. Emily Brontë, *Wuthering Heights* (1847; rpt. New York: W. W. Norton, 1963), p. 264. Future references to this edition will appear in the text.
6. Lionel Trilling, *Sincerity and Authenticity* (Cambridge, Mass.: Harvard University Press, 1972), p. 10.
7. Ariès, *Hour of Our Death*, p. 543, suggests that in the nineteenth century, with the waning of orthodox faith, the cult of the dead which honed life to its greatest intensity became "the only authentic religion."
8. Bram Dijkstra, for instance, sees nothing but "morbid eroticism" in the many paintings of dying women he displays and excoriates; see his *Idols of Perversity: Fantasies of Feminine Evil in Fin-de-Siècle Culture* (New York and Oxford: Oxford University Press, 1986), esp. pp. 25–63.
9. T. A. Palmer, *East Lynne*, in *Nineteenth-Century British Drama*, ed. Leonard R. N. Ashley (Glenview, Ill.: Scott, Foresman and Co., 1967), p. 396. First performance 1874.
10. Ellen Wood, *East Lynne* (1861; rpt. New Brunswick, N.J.: Rutgers University Press, 1984), pp. 518–519.
11. Charlotte Brontë, "Biographical Notice of Ellis and Acton Bell," in *Wuthering Heights*, p. 7.
12. Elizabeth Gaskell, *The Life of Charlotte Brontë* (1857; rpt. Middlesex: Penguin Books, 1975), p. 524.
13. Bram Stoker, *Dracula* (1897; rpt. New York: Bantam Classics, 1981), p. 228; my italics.

14. Ruth Richardson, *Death, Dissection and the Destitute* (London and New York: Routledge & Kegan Paul, 1987), pp. 16–17.

15. Leopold Lewis, *The Bells: Henry Irving and The Bells*, ed. David Mayer (Manchester: Manchester University Press, 1980), act III, p. 76.

16. John Forster, *The Life of Charles Dickens*, 2 vols. (1872–1874; rpt. London: J. M. Dent & Sons, Everyman's Library, 1948), II, 361. Future references to this edition will appear in the text.

17. "The Passing of Arthur," *Idylls of the King*, ed. J. M. Gray (1858–1885; rpt. New Haven and London: Yale University Press, 1983), ll. 366–372, p. 298.

18. Henry Irving's King in Comyns Carr's *King Arthur* (1895) is more conventionally heroic. After his supposed death, he returns to his Court in disguise to kill Mordred (who has assumed the crown and has designs upon the Queen) and to be assured that Guinevere and Lancelot adore him suitably. Unlike Malory's Arthur, and Tennyson's, he fails to assassinate Mordred—Lancelot must finish that job for him offstage—but he does die in Court, much wept over. Moreover, his command to throw Excalibur in the lake is obeyed at once. Excalibur's disappearance is no longer an elegy, but a stirring tribute to the British Navy, providing Comyns Carr with his militaristic refrain: "the sword is in the sea." When he played King Arthur, Irving was campaigning for his knighthood; therefore he could not die without doing so patriotically. But Tennyson's theatrical instinct is sounder than Comyns Carr's. His King's sanctified but ineffectual life is a tribute to the galvanizing power of death, the true hero of the *Idylls*.

19. *Gondal's Queen, A Novel in Verse, by Emily Jane Brontë*, arranged by Fannie E. Ratchford (1955; rpt. Austin and London: University of Texas Press, 1977), p. 160.

20. Garrett Stewart, *Death Sentences: Styles of Dying in British Fiction* (Cambridge, Mass.: Harvard University Press, 1984), p. 19.

21. "This ability to die and yet somehow remain alive was for Dickens the chief attraction of 'the jocund world of pantomime,' where 'there is no affliction or calamity that leaves the least impression,'" Edwin M. Eigner, *The Dickens Pantomime* (Berkeley and Los Angeles: University of California Press, 1989), p. 160. Eigner quotes Dickens' "A Curious Dance Round a Curious Tree."

22. See E. F. Bleiler's introductions to *Five Victorian Ghost Novels* (New York: Dover Publications, 1971), p. v, and *The Collected Ghost Stories of Mrs. J. H. Riddell* (New York: Dover Publications, 1977), pp. xxiii-xxiv.

23. See E. F. Bleiler's introduction to M. R. James, *Ghost Stories of an Antiquary* (New York: Dover Publications, 1971), p. 5.

24. *The Complete Poems of Thomas Hardy*, ed. James Gibson (London: Macmillan, 1976), p. 861.

25. Lord Dunsany, *The Last Book of Wonder* (Boston: John W. Luce & Co., 1916), p. 8.

26. Charles Dickens, *A Christmas Carol* (1843), in *A Christmas Carol and Other Victorian Fairy Tales*, ed. U. C. Knoepflmacher (New York: Bantam Classics, 1983), p. 16.

27. Jack Sullivan, *Elegant Nightmares: The English Ghost Story from LeFanu to Blackwood* (Athens: Ohio University Press, 1978), pp. 133–134.

28. Quoted in Peter Gunn, *Vernon Lee: Violet Paget, 1856–1935* (London: Oxford University Press, 1964), p. 129.

29. Henry James, *The Turn of the Screw* (1898; rpt. New York: W. W. Norton, 1966), pp. 24, 52.

30. Vernon Lee, "A Phantom Lover," in Bleiler, *Five Victorian Ghost Novels*, pp. 330–31.

## Epilogue: Theatrical Fears

1. Gordon Craig, *Henry Irving* (New York and Toronto: Longmans, Green and Co., 1930), pp. 220–221; ellipsis Craig's.

2. For an account of some female theatrical managers, see Nina Auerbach, *Ellen Terry, Player in Her Time* (New York: W. W. Norton, 1987), pp. 57–60.

3. See, for instance, Michael Baker's paradigmatically titled *The Rise of the Victorian Actor* (Totowa, N.J.: Rowman & Littlefield, 1978).

# · ILLUSTRATION SOURCES ·

Frontispiece: Vignette, *Measure for Measure, Shakespeare's Plays: with his Life,* ed. Guilian C. Verplanck, Ltd., 3 vols., II, the comedies (New York: Harper & Brothers, 1847). Page 1: *A Midsommer Nights Dreame,* illustrated by J. Moyr Smith (London: Bernard Quaritch, 1892). Page 19: Ellen Terry as Puck. Ellen Terry, *Ellen Terry's Memoirs,* with a Preface, Notes, and Additional Biographical Material by Edith Craig and Christopher St. John, 1932 (reprint, New York: Benjamin Blom, 1969). Page 53: Vignette, *King Lear, Shakespeare's Plays: with his Life,* ed. Guilian C. Verplanck, Ltd., 3 vols., III, the tragedies (New York: Harper & Brothers, 1847). Page 85: Johnston Forbes-Robertson as the ghost in *Hamlet,* 1888 (Special Collections, Van Pelt Library, University of Pennsylvania). Page 111: Vignette, *A Midsummer Night's Dream,* by William Shakespeare (New York: E. P. Dutton & Co., 1890).

All illustrations are reproduced by courtesy of the Furness Collection, Special Collections, Van Pelt Library, University of Pennsylvania.

# · INDEX ·

# Index

# Index

Gothicism: in Victorian England, 64–65, 66, 70–71, 76–83, 93–94, 101–109; in the twentieth century, 101. *See also* Novel

Hardy, Thomas, 37, 99, 102
Harman, Barbara, 123n18
Hazlewood, C. H. *See* Braddon
Heroes, in Victorian culture, 10, 12, 30–31, 61–63, 67–68, 98, 106; Shakespeare as, 6–8; and biography, 17–18, 37, 42, 72, 78–79; women as, 23, 67–70, 83; Irving as, 77–80, 95–97, 125n18. *See also* Biography; Carlyle; Sincerity; Theatricality
Hitchcock, Alfred, *Psycho*, 101

Irving, Henry, 77–80, 81, 82, 95, 96, 97, 106, 113–114; in *The Bells*, 77, 78, 95; in *King Arthur*, 97, 125n18

James, Henry, 13; *The Turn of the Screw*, 45–46, 104–108; "The Jolly Corner," mentioned, 104
James, M. R., 44–45, 102

Kean, Edmund, 36
King, Stephen, *Salem's Lot*, 101
Kingsley, Charles, 3
Kipling, Rudyard: "'They,'" 24–25, 31; *Kim*, 27, 46; *Jungle Books*, 46

Lateau, Louise, 82, 83
Lee, Vernon (Violet Paget), *Hauntings*, 104; "A Phantom Lover," 104–109; "Prince Alberic and the Snake Lady," "Amour Dure," mentioned, 108
Lewes, George Henry, 118n12
Levine, George, 57
Life, cycle of, Victorian representations of, 3–4, 17–18, 89–90, 109, 114. *See also* Biography; Faith

MacDonald, George, 46
Mackail, Denis, quoted, 49

Marriage, Victorian representations of, 62–66, 67, 68, 72
Marshall, David, quoted, 60–61
"Master Betty," 35–36, 37
Mazer, Cary M., quoted, 80
Meisel, Martin, 32
Melodrama, 15–17, 46
Millais, John Everett, *The Drowning of Ophelia*, 90

Newman, John Henry, *Apologia Pro Vita Sua*, 3, 4, 18
Nightingale, Florence, 66
Novel: in Victorian England, 17, 21, 76, 80; and selfhood, 27, 43, 78; of development, 27–28, 62–64, 66; in the eighteenth century, 60–61; Gothic, 64–65, 66, 70–71, 76–83, 93–94, 101–109

*Once Upon a Time There Were Two Kings* (extravaganza), 58
Onions, Oliver, "The Last Thyrsus," 64–65; "The Beckoning Fair One," 104, 106

Painting, in the nineteenth century, 90; theatricality of, 13
Palmer, T. A. *See* Wood
Pantomime, 14–15, 31, 34, 36, 46, 49, 57–58, 102, 103, 125n21. *See also* Theater; Theatricality
Planché, James Robinson, *The Island of Jewels* (extravaganza), 15
Poetry, death in Victorian, 98–100

Richardson, Ruth, quoted, 94
Riddell, Charlotte, 44
Robertson, Tom, *Caste*, 33–34
Rossetti, Christina: *Goblin Market*, 46; "When I Am Dead . . . ," 99–100
Rossetti, Dante Gabriel, *Beata Beatrix*, 90

# Index